D0403490

STUDIES IN MODERN EUROPEAN
LITERATURE AND THOUGHT

General Editor:

ERICH HELLER

*Professor of German
in the University College of Swansea*

TOLSTOY

TOLSTOY

BY

THEODORE REDPATH

BOWES & BOWES
LONDON

© Theodore Redpath 1960

SBN 370 00216 4

Second edition, 1969
First published in 1960 in the Series
Studies in Modern European Literature and Thought
by Bowes and Bowes Publishers Ltd,
9 Bow Street, London, WC2
Printed in Great Britain by
Fletcher & Son Ltd, Norwich
Set in Monotype Garamond

CONTENTS

PREFACE TO THE FIRST IMPRESSION

This little book is a brief survey of Tolstoy's thought and fiction. It is intended primarily for the general reader rather than for the Slavonic specialist. I have, however, assumed that the reader has read *War and Peace* and *Anna Karenina*, and knows the rough outline of Tolstoy's life.

I have hoped that my book may achieve several objects: that it may help to stir readers to read more of Tolstoy; that it may contribute to the understanding and true assessment of his work as a thinker and writer of fiction; that it may stimulate readers to face the real challenge offered by Tolstoy's ideas on life and civilization; and that it may suggest some lines of interest and inquiry concerning Tolstoy's work, which readers may find it worthwhile to pursue further.

To facilitate further reading and study I have compiled a Select Bibliography, which I have had to keep very short, and which I have been asked to restrict, with a few exceptions, to works in English. I have, however, written a short note on some of the more important of the recent Russian work on Tolstoy. I have also from time to time indicated in footnotes material for further study on particular points, and I have occasionally included references to some of the many books and articles only available as yet in Russian, in the hope that these references may be of use to the growing number of general readers who have acquired some knowledge of the Russian language.

I gratefully acknowledge suggestions, help and encouragement from my friends Prof. Dr. T. B. Balta, Dr. M. Markovitch, Dr. G. von Hippel, Dr.

H. Ben-Israel, Mr. L. G. Salingar, and Mr. M. Wykes-Joyce. I also thank Prof. N. K. Gudzy of Moscow University for information about recent work on Tolstoy, and for sending me a collection of essays.

THEODORE REDPATH

Cambridge
January 1959.

PREFACE TO THE SECOND IMPRESSION

I have been asked to limit corrections to a minimum, and this I have readily done. I should not wish to tinker with work which was of a piece when I wrote it. In any case, however, my attitudes to Tolstoy, his ideas and his work do not seem to have changed substantially during the last ten years, except perhaps that I admire non-violent resistance to aggression more than I did, though mainly in cases where violent resistance would very probably be futile.

On the other hand, I have added on pp. 127–8 a Supplementary Select Bibliography, listing books (including *collections* of articles but not single articles) published up till 1968. I hope this may be found useful.

THEODORE REDPATH

Cambridge
March 1969

INTRODUCTION

It is just over a century since Tolstoy published his first work, and nearly half a century since he died. It is clear enough that he is a great writer and personality, but perhaps not wholly clear wherein the greatness of his achievement lies. To some he has seemed a great artist gone astray, who, after writing *War and Peace* in his thirties and *Anna Karenina* in his forties, not only turned his back on art, but pretentiously set himself up as a great thinker, while in reality his ideas have little claim to serious consideration. To others—and these have accepted Tolstoy's own ultimate evaluation—his work as a moral and religious teacher in his last thirty-two years, both in direct and in fictional form, has appeared immeasurably more important not only than *Childhood*, *Boyhood*, and *The Cossacks*, but even than the novels on which his reputation now generally rests. These are two extreme views. Various medial attitudes have also been adopted. In recent years there has been, on the whole, a tendency to neglect or depreciate Tolstoy the thinker as contrasted with Tolstoy the artist. There have been several causes of this tendency, chief among which, perhaps, have been increased knowledge of Tolstoy's personal life and family conflicts, and an inclination, fostered by the spread of psychology and, in particular, of psychoanalysis, to 'explain' (and ultimately to discount) world-views by tracing them to their psychological sources.

Should we value Tolstoy more as artist or as thinker: and how much more? Should we take one of the extreme views, or does the truth lie in some more complex and discriminating estimate? And, if so, what precisely should this estimate be? These are among the questions which I shall eventually try to answer.

My main concern, however, will be briefly to review Tolstoy's ideas and fiction. I shall only concentrate on his life, character, or personality where they throw light on the fiction and ideas.

My chapter on Tolstoy's ideas comes first because recently these have received less attention than his fiction, life, and character. Though some of the ideas are patently absurd, many still demand an answer and not merely a dismissal or evasion by such means as psychological explanation. Tolstoy himself offered his ideas for serious consideration. They were taken on their merits both by disciples, like Gandhi, and by repudiators, like the Russian Orthodox Church. His value as a thinker, moreover, depends on the value of his ideas. It would therefore seem more appropriate to attempt a plain review of these ideas than to treat them merely as emanations or manoeuvrings—which they may also be—of a complex and tragic personality.

The ideas treated will be almost entirely ideas elaborated by Tolstoy after his 'conversion' in 1878, for it is these he chiefly valued, and these that have brought him fame and notoriety as a thinker. (I have excluded his ideas on Education, which were elaborated earlier.) It is important to realize, however, that, although elaborated after 1878, many of these ideas occur in earlier works, letters, diaries and notebooks, though often all but lost among extraneous and even conflicting thoughts. Again, Tolstoy's ideas on some topics (e.g. immortality and marriage) either changed entirely or fluctuated during his later years. Such changes will require brief mention. Many of his main ideas, however, remained substantially unchanged for the last thirty years of his life; and it is these that will form the staple of the first chapter.

In my chapter on Tolstoy's fiction I try briefly to describe and revaluate much of Tolstoy's fiction, and to indicate its general evolution. My treatment of the better-known works assumes that the reader is acquainted with them. Genetic interpretation will be used for certain works on which it seems to throw particular light. I have excluded Tolstoy's dramas. Though one or two of his plays have definite merit, Tolstoy, as he well knew, was not at his best in drama ('sculptor's work', he called it), which allowed little scope for two of his strongest talents: for observation and analysis of the stream of consciousness, and for minute physical description.

My third chapter is intended to indicate some of the features of Tolstoy's life and character which caused or appreciably affected his ideas and fiction. Knowledge of Tolstoy's life and character is often peculiarly relevant to understanding and evaluating his ideas and work. I place this chapter third, because I believe that it is usually more illuminating to discuss a writer's ideas and work first, and only to suggest causal explanations after that.

In a brief Conclusion I offer a general assessment of Tolstoy as thinker and writer of fiction. There is a far better chance of making a valid assessment than there was forty years ago, that is, at the centenary of Tolstoy's birth. We have, thanks to the remarkable work of Soviet scholars and critics,[1] much more material to draw on than was then available, though scarcely any of this fresh material has yet been translated into any of the languages of Western Europe, and very limited use has yet been made of it in Western criticism.[2]

[1] A brief note on some of the most important of this work will be found on pp. 116–18. See also pp. 127–8.
[2] There are, however, exceptions, e.g. Ernest Simmons's biography, *Leo Tolstoy*, London, 1949, R. F. Christian's *Tolstoy's 'War and Peace'*, Oxford, 1962, Henri Troyat's *Tolstoï*, Paris, 1965 (Eng. tr., London, 1968), John Bayley's *Tolstoy and the Novel*, London, 1966, and G. W. Spence's *Tolstoy the Ascetic*, Edinburgh, 1967.

I

The Realm of Ideas

ON RELIGION

> What a divine religion might be found out, if
> charity were really made the principle of it, instead
> of faith.
>
> Shelley.

A conversation about religion while a young officer
at the Siege of Sevastopol suggested to Tolstoy the
idea of founding 'a new religion corresponding to
the present state of mankind: the religion of Christ
but purged of dogmas and mysteriousness—a practical religion, not promising future bliss but bringing
about bliss on earth'.[1] He felt capable of devoting his
whole life to this idea. For over twenty years other
aims dominated him; but then the idea arose again,
and became the inspiration of his last thirty-two
years.

Tolstoy's desire for an undogmatic, rational, ethical
Christianity directed and sustained his extensive theo-
logical researches in the early 1880s, including his
work on the New Testament and his scrutiny of the
dogmas of the Russian Orthodox Church. He con-
cluded that the Church had accepted many absurd and
un-Christian doctrines, which it could only impose
on people because it was powerful—the Church being
simply 'Power in the hands of certain men',[2] working
mainly through hypnotic devices, but always able to
invoke open coercion.

Doctrines Tolstoy thought absurd included the
Fall, the scheme of Atonement and Redemption, the

---

[1] *Diary*, 5 March 1855.
[2] *The Kingdom of God is Within You*, Centenary Edition (hereafter referred to as *CE*), *20*, 99.

Trinity, and the idea that Christ was *the* son of God, so that nobody else could be a 'Son of God' in the same sense. He believed that these doctrines had been superimposed on the true teaching of Christ by St. Paul and other theologians. He was indignant at this perversion of Christianity, because he thought Christ the greatest religious teacher so far, and religion the greatest thing in the world. The strength of Christ's teaching lay in his moral precepts, designed to establish the Kingdom of God in this world. The accretions begun by St. Paul (including the doctrine of personal immortality) [1] had converted Christianity into a religion of personal salvation in another world. The alien doctrine of the Fall had been introduced, and then emphasized by the Churches, who thus 'shut out ethics', and made men 'mere spectators' of their own redemption. Priests thus acquired the position of intermediaries with the redeemer, and instituted the sacraments and external observances typical of religions in decline.

Christ's true teaching, in Tolstoy's view, was partly identical with that of Moses, Confucius, Laotse, Buddha, and Socrates, but made further advances. Chief of these was the doctrine that men should not resist evil by violence. In *What I Believe* [2] Tolstoy tells us that it was the injunction in the Sermon on the Mount not to resist evil but to turn the other cheek (Matt. v. 38, 39) that 'enabled him to understand the whole Christian teaching'. The true meaning of the injunction was that no violence of any sort should ever be used to resist evil. In teaching this, Christ was a great innovator, and a real menace to the established order of his time, so that it was no wonder the Jews had him killed. A sincere believer in Christ's doctrine would not only forgo

[1] Later Tolstoy came to believe in some kind of survival of the spiritual part of each individual, and sometimes referred to death as a mere illusion.
[2] *CE, II.*

private revenge, but renounce the courts, and refuse to fight in a war. Christ also taught: (1) that one should never be angry with anyone (Matt. v. 21–6); (2) that no one should divorce for any cause (31–2); (3) that no one should ever take an oath, e.g. of allegiance (33–7); (4) that one should love the enemies of the state to which one happens to belong (43–8). Tolstoy gives detailed arguments for these interpretations.

To follow these precepts of Christ would mean the Kingdom of God on earth. But they had been too radical not only for the Jews, but for the established order ever since. Ecclesiastics had therefore blunted their edge by interpretation and interpolation. St. John Chrysostom, for instance, had taught that the *lex talionis* was so reasonable that Christ could not have meant to reject it.[1] Indeed, the general view of the Churches had been that Christ had not rejected but confirmed the Mosaic law. But the *true* moral teaching of Christ was a remarkable advance on the Mosaic law, and, indeed, the greatest moral teaching the world had ever known.

Tolstoy did not, however, think of Christ's teaching as merely moral. He recognized it as religious. A true Christian life involved trying to get continually clearer as to God's purpose, and attempting to promote it in the world. According to Tolstoy only three types of attitude to life are possible: (1) the *egoistic*—trying to gratify one's own will exclusively; (2) the *social*—trying to gratify the will of one's family, tribe, race or nation, or of humanity as a whole; (3) the *Christian*—trying to fulfil the will of God, and sacrificing one's personality, and the welfare of one's family, tribe, race, or nation to that end. The history and true destiny of humanity consisted in passing from the egoistic to the Christian attitude. Comtian positivism and Huxleyan humanitarianism,

[1] See St. John Chrysostom, *Homilies on the Gospel of Matthew*, pt. I, Hom. xvi (Pusey's Library of the Fathers, 236–7).

no less than patriotism and doctrines of racial superiority, sprang from attitudes of the social type. (Humanitarianism was, besides, in Tolstoy's view, vague and unsatisfactory. 'Humanity is a fiction and it is impossible to love it.')[1] A moral doctrine based on the Darwinian conception of a struggle for existence would spring from either an egoistic or a social attitude. Spiritualism arose from an egoistic attitude.

Tolstoy was at pains to show that the Christian attitude was eminently reasonable. In his elaborate and profound essay *On Life*,[2] starting from an assumption like Hobbes's, that each man lives only for his own good or happiness, Tolstoy suggests that, when a man realizes the world is full of other beings like himself, he cannot help thinking they wish to destroy him to achieve their aims. Life then seems a great evil. Moreover, the longer a man lives the more clearly he sees that enjoyments continually dwindle, while weariness, satiety, troubles, and suffering increase. Finally, there is the inexorable approach of death, which will totally destroy his individual life and every chance of personal welfare. Once a man sees all this, he cannot get it out of his mind. He is haunted by life's basic contradiction: that each man wants personal welfare, but cannot attain it. It was this contradiction the great moral teachers had tried to solve—by discovering a welfare indestructible by strife, sufferings, or death. Human progress had consisted in attaining an ever clearer vision of this welfare. Christ's vision, the highest yet, was that it lay in loving God and other people, and subordinating one's 'animal personality' to this love. This was eminently reasonable, since it completely solved the contradiction of life. It would eliminate strife, since no one who loves God and other people would ever

---

[1] *The Kingdom of God is Within You, CE, 20*, 126.
[2] *CE, 12*.

try to benefit at the expense of his fellow men. Moreover, for a man who understands that his true life consists in loving, not in 'animal welfare', sufferings and death will no longer hold any terror.

In a later essay, *What is Religion?* (1902),[1] Tolstoy warns against a new threat to reasonable views on life: the widespread acceptance of 'the ravings of Herr Nietzsche'. This 'bold but limited and abnormal German' offered the advice: 'Live as you please, paying no attention to the lives of others'. This was not merely anti-Christian, as Nietzsche knew, but contrary to the moral teaching of all the great religions—subjection of the passions and self-renunciation.

These are some of Tolstoy's main religious ideas. They and many others are expressed richly and forcibly in many non-fictional works and essays,[2] and in his later fiction, especially *Resurrection* (1899); while in his stirring *Confession* (1879)[3] he recounts his passage into his final, religious, phase.

The promulgation of Tolstoy's religious ideas led to his virtual excommunication by the Orthodox Church (1901); but anti-religious thinkers also attacked them.

For those of us who have no great confidence in another life, but a serious concern with life here and now, Tolstoy's desire for a religion aiming at bliss on earth has natural appeal. Yet Tolstoy's own religion, though noble, is too limited. The world is mysterious, and perplexing, and a religion should reflect this. Tolstoy's *art*, both before and after his conversion, often does, but his *religion*, though *mystic* in its intimate sense of the direct relationship of the in-

[1] *CE, 12.*
[2] Many of these appear in *CE, 11, 12, 14, 20* and *21*. Others, including *A Critique of Dogmatic Theology* and *An Examination of the four Gospels*, are included in Leo Wiener's translation (see Bibliography).
[3] *CE, 11.*

dividual to God, does not show enough awareness of the world's *mysteriousness*.

Tolstoy's searching analysis of the 'degeneration' of Christ's teaching into the dogmas of the Churches has force; but he was not alive enough to the beauty or value of religious myths, and he failed to consider the possibility of figurative interpretation of the doctrines he found absurd, let alone the subtler question of the relationship between figurative and literal interpretation. Some of us may find it exceedingly hard to believe in such doctrines as the divinity of Christ, the Fall, or the physical resurrection of Christ, but we can still admire these doctrines for a certain splendour, however alien to us, and we are not even bound to deny the value of believing in them for those who can. Moreover, though some Christian dogmas seem scarcely susceptible of anything but literal interpretation, e.g. the physical Resurrection of Christ, many are amenable to figurative interpretation, and so taken it is hard to maintain that they are 'absurd'. Again, in the case of some dogmas the distinction between figurative and literal interpretation ceases to be significant. If, for instance, such an exacting doctrine as transubstantiation is not absurd in a figurative sense, how can it be so literally, since it holds that the phenomena characteristic of the bread and wine remain? *Credo quia non absurdum est* would, however, be a poor position; and, in any case, one can at least understand that the morally earnest Tolstoy should have been indignant at doctrines he considered to have smudged the greatest religious teaching in the world, and delayed its reception by many centuries. Yet he evidently underrated the amount of value and even truth latent in the startling doctrines and forms of ecclesiastical Christianity.

As to Tolstoy's own interpretation of Christ's teaching, it is hard to estimate its truth. Whether, for instance, Christ really taught non-resistance to evil by violence has sharply divided theologians, and may even be an insoluble question. Yet whether St. John Chrysostom and the other theologians who rejected pacifism interpreted right or not, I cannot help thinking they were wise. However admirable the moral integrity of doing no violence, to maintain that it is paramount involves admitting that we should offer no violence even were the very worst people to hold the very best in complete worldly subjection of the most ignominious kind. Some of us cannot make such an admission.

Tolstoy's classification of attitudes to life is illuminating; but both it and the doctrine he bases on it seem too rigid. He does not see that it might be God's will that a man should often aim at gratifying his own will. He is a far cry from the opinion of our sensible Christian philosopher, Bishop Butler, that there was not too much but too little self-love in the world,[1] and that, though conscience was a regulating principle placed in authority over egoistic and social impulses, those dynamic urges were each allowable within due limits.[2] Tolstoy's views here insult the selfhood of men; while his views on certain other matters are, contrariwise, based on a touching but misguided faith (confirmed if not initiated by the potent influence of Rousseau)[3] in the 'natural' *goodness* of human nature. Tolstoy's thought is, indeed, riddled with inconsistencies deriving from his adherence to two opposite views of human nature: (1) that men are fundamentally egoistic, and egoistic impulses bad; and (2) that men are fundamentally good. Tolstoy is also unjust to social impulses. These often serve constructive purposes, such as a sane religion might well consider in accord with the will of God. It is, however, clear enough

[1] *Sermons on Human Nature*, ed. W. R. Matthews, London, 1914, reprd. 1953, 24.
[2] Ibid., 33–45.
[3] For a thorough and discriminating study of the immense influence of Rousseau on Tolstoy's thought see Milan Markovitch, *Jean-Jacques Rousseau et Tolstoï*, Paris, 1928.

that action from egoistic or social impulses will not infallibly be right, whereas action in accordance with the will of an infinitely good God *could never be wrong*.

Tolstoy's proof of the *reasonableness* of the Christian attitude is shaky. The assumption of psychological egoism is an uncertain foundation for argument, since it does not, of itself, specify wherein individuals take their good or happiness to lie. For each man to live exclusively 'for his own good' need not involve conflict, and even where conflict occurred individuals might modify their conception of the 'good' they wanted. Hobbes saw this, and his enlightened egoist is very civil and reasonable. Nor would a man in a world of egoists necessarily conceive it as Tolstoy said he would—as a world of fierce competition, with everyone ready to destroy his fellows. Tolstoy's view is tainted with Schopenhauerian pessimism. So is his generalization on the ills of advancing years. Death will come for all, but it may not end all personal welfare, and, even if it did, individual life would not be nugatory. It has, indeed, been an assumption in some of the greatest religions and philosophies that only the permanent is really important; but that is by no means self-evident. In any case, Tolstoy's conclusions in *On Life* rest on the assumption that each man lives for his own good or happiness, and that assumption many philosophers have questioned or even denied. Furthermore, Tolstoy has failed to show that such personal welfare is unattainable in this life. Thus both sides of his basic contradiction are rather frail figures. Yet if even one collapsed, the contradiction would vanish also.

Finally, Tolstoy seems to have distorted the gospel of love. Christ's second commandment, *Love thy neighbour as thyself*, does not demand the annihilation of personal desire. Indeed, if we had no personal desires, how could those who love us show their love to the full?

Comparison of the ideas of Tolstoy and Nietzsche is exciting and fruitful,[1] but here my concern is only with Tolstoy's warning against Nietzsche's teaching of egotism. I believe the views of Tolstoy and Nietzsche can be regarded as opposite reactions to the Schopenhauerian pessimism which so strongly impressed both of them, and that both their reactions are vitiated by the fine though false philosophy they were trying to answer while accepting some of its basic assumptions. If the world is not so bad as Schopenhauer felt, and if there is real hope for the earthly welfare of a society of human beings with rich and strong personal desires, then neither the utter self-renunciation of Tolstoy nor the exaggerated egotism and forced optimism of Nietzsche are appropriate as general philosophies of life.

ON POLITICS AND SOCIAL ETHICS

Anarchy follows certainly from Christianity in its application to social life.

Tolstoy, in conversation with A. B. Goldenweizer (1908).

The mature Tolstoy taught anarchism. A government was 'a set of men who do violence to others'.[2] Despotisms, constitutional monarchies, republics, differed only in the number of oppressors and the crudity of the violence. All private property, privileges, and exclusive social pleasures depended upon the existence of violent means (e.g. police, law courts,

[1] For brief comparison of Tolstoy and Nietzsche see J. Lavrin, *Tolstoy: an approach*, London, 1944, 1948, ch. XII, and Prof. Lavrin's article 'Tolstoy and Nietzsche', *Slavonic Review*, June 1925, 67–82. For a fuller discussion see L. Shestov, *Dobro v uchenii Tolstovo i Nietzsche*, Berlin, 1923 (tr. into German as *Tolstoi und Nietzsche*, Köln, 1923, and into French as L. Chestov, *L'idée de bien chez Tolstoï et chez Nietzsche*, Paris, 1949). See also H. E. Davis, *Tolstoy & Nietzsche*, New York, 1929.
[2] *The Kingdom of God is Within You, CE, 20, 176.*

armies) of repressing interference with them. Governments might have been of some use in an era of great individual violence, but individual tendencies to violence had decreased, while governments had grown more powerful, and so more corrupt and coercive. To say that states were needed to enable the good to restrain the bad was to beg the question by assuming that those in power were good. It is not the good who rule, but proud, cunning and cruel men, who seize power and hang on to it for themselves and their descendants. To speak of Christians ruling seemed even ridiculous. 'Christianity in its true sense puts an end to the state. It was so understood from its very beginning, and for that Christ was crucified.' [1]

It was not the state but public opinion that protected against internal violence. Moreover, state punishment only brutalized, and increased delinquency. Nor was the state required as purveyor of religion or culture, or of communications or other amenities. In any case, all states usually did was interfere—as over the abolition of corporal punishment, torture, and slavery, and the establishment of a free press and the right of public meeting. Again, it was self-refuting to defend the state as a guarantee against enslavement by neighbouring states. Its armed forces were a cause of internal enslavement. Moreover, as Montesquieu had said, the increase of armies is infectious. Universal conscription had now been adopted in a number of European countries. And in Germany and the U.S.A., as the solidarity of the workers increased, so did the demand of the ruling classes for a larger army, even though no foreign attack was threatened. Universal conscription was the *reductio ad absurdum* of the 'social' conception of life. All citizens were now under arms to uphold all the injustices inflicted on them; and so had become their own oppressors.

[1] *The Kingdom of God is Within You, CE, 20,* 281.

Conscription was thus the keystone of the modern state. But Christianity demanded conscientious objection, which was already increasing, and would gather momentum, until government collapsed. The end of government would be hastened by the increase in Christian objections to oaths of allegiance, payment of taxes, and legal proceedings. No wonder governments had taken alarm. They knew how to deal with socialists, communists, and anarchistic terrorists; but were helpless against Christianity, which would sap them from within.

A true Christian would, however, be as averse to revolution as to government. Tolstoy, though strongly sympathetic towards the workers, was deeply opposed to the social revolutionary movements of his time, and was sharply attacked by Marxists, including Lenin and Plekhanov.[1] For them he represented the retrograde idea of patriarchal peasantry, and by his idea of non-resistance discouraged radical political action.

Tolstoy's sympathies with the workers, on the other hand, were as strong as even an exacting Marxist could desire. He considered them economic slaves, cheated of their rightful inheritance. His most detailed analysis of the contemporary economic and social situation is in *What Then Must We Do?* [2] (completed 1886), where he also proposes his remedies. This powerful work sprang from Tolstoy's horror at the poverty and squalor he found in Moscow in 1881, when he went from the country to live there. He sought the causes, and his conclusion was that the main cause was the drift of wealth from country to town. Each autumn the great wealth of the crops was in the villages; but through taxation, requisitioning,

[1] Some of the most important of the articles by Lenin and Plekhanov are included in *L. N. Tolstoy v russkoy kritike*, ed. S. P. Bychkov, Moscow, 1952. See also *Tolstoi im Spiegel des Marxismus*, Wien—Berlin, 1928, and *International Literature*, 1934, No. 6.
[2] *CE, 14.*

rents, the temptation of vodka, weddings, fêtes, ped-
lars, it passed to the small towns, to dealers, landowners, officials, and manufacturers, who took it to
the big cities to enjoy it. Many villagers flocked after
them, partly to avoid starvation, partly for luxury
and easy money. Some succeeded there, like the
rich, in working less and exploiting others more;
others fared moderately; while others broke down,
lost the habit of work, and filled the brothels and
doss-houses. The rich lavished care and money on
segregating themselves from the poor. A *nouveau-
riche* would first separate himself from the kitchen
and servants, then adopt exclusive manners and
clothes, and get more servants as a barrier against the
poor. Cleanliness and education served the same purpose of segregation. The rich wanted to prevent the
poor seeing how they enjoyed themselves: 'but to
hide is impossible, and they do see'.[1] Sometimes the
rich tried to salve their consciences with charity,
which meant 'chucking away farthings with one
hand . . . while gathering thousands from the poor
with the other'.[2] The peasants who stayed in the villages at least retained their ideal of industrious work;
but they did not receive their rights—to reap the full
value of the land. They had to pay rent to a so-called
'owner', taxes to the state, and hire-money to capitalists for tools and machinery. This forced them to
sell their produce at less than its worth, and to continue slaving to make ends meet. Serfs had, indeed,
been 'emancipated' in 1861; but that only meant the
replacement of personal by economic slavery. Those
who had money could twist those who had none into
ropes. This was slavery, and it was protected by
armed forces.

As remedies, besides the dissolution of these
armed forces, Tolstoy proposed that people should
get off the backs of the poor by ceasing to own land,

[1] *What Then Must We Do? CE, 14*, 87.
[2] Ibid., 95.

accept government employment, and use money. It would mean people restricting their needs, and doing more for themselves. This would check the drift to the towns, since the demand for urban labour would vanish. Segregation from the workers would cease; for all would be workers. The privileged, in forgoing their privileges, would also lose their shame. The privilege of freedom from manual toil could only be justified if the privileged either (1) had special functions, or (2) did work so useful to all that it compensated for the extra burden on others. In pre-Christian times the privileged asserted they were a race apart, appointed by God to rule or teach. Christianity, maintaining the equality and unity of all men, excluded this justification. So new justifications were devised. Hegel (according to Tolstoy's inadequate interpretation) held that whatever is is reasonable and that the state is needed to perfect personality. Malthusians had contended that the squalor of the workers was their own fault for being so stupid as to be born when they knew they would have nothing to eat. People now said the privileged were compensating humanity by services; but they were not. An activity was only useful if either (1) the 'beneficiary' agreed it was, or (2) the 'benefactor's' motive was altruistic. Now 'government people' (including priests), landowners, industrialists, bankers, merchants, scientists, artists, fulfilled neither condition. Scientists and artists even impudently denied that they need be useful. Yet they had seemingly replaced clergy, government, and army as the dominant order in society. They tried to justify themselves by representing society as an organism, and appealing to a 'division of labour' between muscular and brain workers. The inventor of this new creed was Auguste Comte, and its 'Basil the Great', Herbert Spencer. It was built on sand, for society was not an organism. Moreover, even if it were, the *present* division of labour would be questionable. To

27

weave cotton cloth every day one's whole life long was clearly wrong, and this kind of 'division of labour' was simply the result of human oppression. Again, no one deserved freedom from manual work unless others offered him support in return for his special services. If the manual worker were to refuse work without first receiving religious guidance adapted to his reason and conscience, wise government to secure his labour, scientific improvements to facilitate it, and art which he could understand and enjoy, it would be the merest justice; for his work was more important, more essential, than the mental worker's. Actually, the manual workers had fed and clothed the privileged classes, while these had discussed with, and taught and entertained, one another, but forgotten the needs of the manual workers altogether. Men with a real calling to serve others would live among the manual workers. Such men would not need elegant luxuries. Their lives would be as simple as those of the workers themselves.

Tolstoy foresaw that the social malady would probably not be treated by his remedies, but by violent revolution. The thought of this violence horrified him; and he also considered it futile. It would merely replace one state by another; and the manual workers would be no better off, for their socialist masters, though in some ways different from capitalists, would resemble them in others, and so the workers themselves would never receive the wealth they deserved.[1]

Tolstoy's anarchy is at best a Utopian impossibility. The simultaneous collapse of all governments would only open careers of crime to predatory individuals and groups. Moreover, these would be met by counterforces, and eventually a state would probably re-emerge. In any case, this simultaneous collapse is most unlikely, and so is such synchroniza-

[1] *Diary*, 3 Aug. 1898.

tion of conscientious objection in various countries as would result in equilibrium. Further, as long as states exist they will probably stamp on conscientious objection when it threatens security, and objection might then slacken. Only in a world state would Tolstoy's anarchy be likely to flourish, and the more it did the more likely would be the reappearance of small states.

Nor has Tolstoy proved anarchy desirable. He has not proved modern governments always or even generally worse than no government. And his refusal to distinguish between good and bad rulers is simply blind. There is Nero, but there is also Augustus. Besides, Tolstoy fails to appreciate that egoists *may* greatly benefit humanity. Yet on his view of Christianity he was right that a true Christian could never rule; since a ruler might always need to use violence to resist evil. Tolstoy's anarchism, in any case, followed from his Christianity, and that is no recommendation of his Christianity. Again, from the ill-effects of state punishments it would not follow that states should be abolished, but only that penal methods should be improved. And was it not states that abolished slavery, and established the rights of free speech and public meeting? And did not states sometimes protect the poor against the rich? Nor is the view that the state protects against enslavement by neighbouring states self-refuting. An especially predatory state (Tolstoy cites contemporary Germany) would surely be less likely to attack and conquer states which were well-armed?[1] Yet Tolstoy suggests the opposite, in an appeal, not to the high principle that it is always better for the good to yield

[1] Machiavelli was surely wiser than Tolstoy in asserting (in the *Discourses on Livy*) that one can fearlessly tyrannize over men who are more inclined to put up with insults than to avenge them? And, if Machiavelli is right, then not to resist will be to encourage tyrants to be tyrannical, which, on Tolstoy's own principles, will be to make them worse than they otherwise would be.

than for them to resist by violence, but merely to worldly wisdom. Tolstoy is in an uneasy position. He wants to encourage pacifism by saying it will work out well in a worldly way; yet he risks forfeiting a mainstay of his anarchism if he weakens his emphasis on the harmfulness of states. What, finally, of Tolstoy's basic assertion that government is 'a set of men who do violence to others'? If we neutralize the emotive charge in the fine polemical term 'violence', does the assertion mean more than that a government is a set of men who make people do things they would not wish to, do to them things they do not like, and prevent them from doing things they would like to do? But if that is what a government is, then it is only always bad if people are always right in what they wish to do, to avoid doing, and to have done to them; and this is hard to believe. It seems also difficult to deny that some of the finest large-scale achievements have resulted from some degree of direct or indirect governmental coercion.

Let us pass from Tolstoy's anarchism to his analysis of the contemporary economic and social situation. This analysis is so anti-capitalistic and so powerful that it is not surprising that in 1910 Lenin recommended the widest publicity for Tolstoy's work, as an aid to preparing the socialist revolution.[1] It is an ironic probability that, despite his uncompromising opposition to social revolution, Tolstoy's work did contribute powerfully to the establishment of Bolshevism.[2]

Tolstoy's analysis is sharp-eyed and factually plausible, but his attitude to the social hierarchy is

[1] Lenin, 'L. N. Tolstoy' in *Sotsial-Demokrat*, No. 18, Nov. 1910; and cf. Lenin's somewhat more critical article 'Tolstoy i proletarskaya borba', *Rabochaya Gazeta*, No. 2, Dec. 1910: both reprinted in *L. N. Tolstoy v russkoy kritike*, ed. S. P. Bychkov, Moscow, 1952, 62–7, 72–4.
[2] See the strong case put by K. S. Laurila in *Tolstois politische Ansichten*, Helsingfors, 1923. See also J. Bourdeau, *Tolstoï, Lénine et La Révolution Russe*, Paris, 1921.

extreme and unacceptable. William Morris's remark that no man is good enough to be another man's master does not prove there should be no masters, for few men are good enough to be other men's servants. And where a man has servants, segregation may make both happier. Moreover, while real oppression is disgusting, few of us do our best without incentive or compulsion. Wanton luxury may be pernicious and even absurd; but many of the graces and subtleties of civilized life, and even many of its noble achievements, would at present be impossible without a solid basis of manual labour, not too amply rewarded. Mechanization of the more unpleasant menial tasks has made some progress. Those not amenable to mechanization could be assigned to a labour service which all would enter for a certain period in life; though the moral advantages of such a system might be outweighed by decreased efficiency. But, in any case, that everyone should be treated alike is a more than dubious principle. Moreover, the relationship of master and servant can be intrinsically noble and satisfying to both parties—which is perhaps why personal loyalty to individual employers is so explicitly discouraged by communists.

Mental workers in Tolstoy's day may often have worked on useless tasks; but Tolstoy's two criteria of utility were hardly valid. Excessive fees may have been asked; but some kinds of useful work may go unperformed without considerable incentives. Tolstoy's thought seems haunted by Proudhon's 'la propriété, c'est le vol'.[1] What is wanted is not these sweeping ideas, but more discrimination.

Yet there are attractions in Tolstoy's dream of country communities, with new folk art to make life

---

[1] Tolstoy had met Proudhon in Brussels in 1861, and been favourably impressed by him. The title of *War and Peace* was suggested by Proudhon's *La Guerre et la Paix*; and, still more important, Tolstoy was greatly indebted to Proudhon for the philosophy of war embodied in the novel (see p. 58, n. 1).

richer and brighter. Here as elsewhere Tolstoy potently influenced the thought of Gandhi.[1] But this noble dream is a dream only. Exploitation, petty enslavement, quarrels, and violence would occur in the actual counterpart of Tolstoy's idealized village. And even the ideal is retrograde. Tolstoy's ideals, in their extremism, go far beyond a healthy decentralization from great industrial areas, and the establishment of mechanized home and village industries. Efficient transport, mechanized agriculture, electric power, and other technical advances would have to be sacrificed. Life would become cramped and monotonous.

The just demands of social conscience and the true remedies for abuses are milder than Tolstoy thought. Reasonable restriction of calls on the work of others; fair wages for the work required; fair work for the wages given; vigorous and fruitful work by the privileged, or at least the preservation of the graces which privilege may bring; abolition of glaring inequalities in capital and income; facilities for rising socially by meritorious achievement; decent personal and industrial relations between employer and worker; fair and uncynical use of armed forces for defence in just wars; respect for the refinements of true culture and civilization—these are less exciting remedies for social and economic abuses than those suggested by Tolstoy or by Communist revolutionaries; but they are more likely to prove satisfactory.

[1] On the relations between Tolstoy and Gandhi see Milan Markovitch, *Tolstoï et Gandhi*, Paris, 1928; and K. Nag, *Tolstoy and Gandhi*, London, 1950. It must be recognized that Tolstoy's teaching of resistance without violence was made politically effective by Gandhi on a very large scale; but it must not be forgotten that the circumstances were very special. Britain had long intended to leave India, and had neither the wish nor the force to be a ruthless occupying power. Moreover, the ideas of Gandhi are already a waning influence in Indian political affairs; and India's whole future, indeed, is highly problematical.

Petrusha. When we grow up we won't learn un-
necessary things.
Volodya. But we will live better ourselves.
Tolstoy, *The Wisdom of Children* (1910).

Tolstoy set little store by natural science. Like
Socrates he thought his contemporaries were neg-
lecting the most important science, moral science.

The intellectuals *said* science should deal with
everything; but that would mean an infinity. What
they *did* was investigate what was easiest or most
gainful. Inanimate objects were easiest. Most gain
came from what served the interests of the ruling
classes, such as armaments, profitable industrial
products, and even the medical science that would
help to heal a few of those who succumbed to
overwork in bad conditions or survived a bout of
slaughter.

Meanwhile the most important matter, *how to be-
have*, was either entrusted to theologians, philosophers, jurists, historians, or political economists, or
else impudently subsumed under some experimental
science. The theologians, and so on, worked to
justify the order which ensured their comforts and
privileges (Hegel was a prime example). The scientists arrogantly claimed they would ultimately
'explain' everything. They even 'explained' what men
should do, namely, fulfil the 'needs' of their organ-
isms, or of the race or species; and the 'needs' were
those conditions the satisfaction of which would
maintain organism, race or species in existence or
fuller activity. Tolstoy thought such ideas unutter-
ably shallow, since they rested on uncritical assumptions which were not 'scientific' but ethical, namely
that existence or fuller activity of individual, race or
species was of paramount importance. Such assumptions sprang from an egoistic or social attitude

to life (cf. p. 17 above). Worst of all was the use of the Darwinian 'struggle for existence' and the idea of artificial selection, as justifications for personal or social conduct. Tolstoy quotes in his *Recollections*[1] a passage from Haeckel justifying capital punishment as not only lightening the 'struggle for existence' for good people, but preventing the transmission of bad qualities to the next generation.[2] In Tolstoy's view the scientific 'justification' is merely a mask for personal views as to who are harmful to the species and what should be done with them—questions which science could not answer.

Practical science had also brought more harm than good. It had given more power to oppressive governments, which were now, in Herzen's phrase, 'Genghiz Khans with telegraph systems'. It had helped to draw workers from the health of the countryside into debilitating factories. Corrupting luxury had multiplied. More powerful weapons of murder had been evolved. No 'victories over nature' could benefit humanity, unless guided by true religious, moral, and social science.

When not harmful, natural science had been useless. It was no use to humanity to know the distance of the earth from the sun; the velocity and frequency of light; the properties of micro-organisms; or to learn about X-rays or that helium had been discovered. Such was the spirit that animated Tolstoy's preface to the translation by his son, Sergei, of Edward Carpenter's essay, *Modern Science: a Criticism*,[3] and that made him call Aristotle, Bacon and Comte, who directed work into natural science, 'unimportant'.[4]

[1] Wr. 1908. Tr. in *CE, 21*.
[2] The passage came from Haeckel's *Natürliche Schöpfungsgeschichte* (in Eng. tr. *The History of Creation*, 4th edn., London, 1892, I, 178).
[3] The preface is translated in *CE, 21*. Carpenter's essay forms part of his *Civilization: its Cause and Cure*.
[4] *On Life, CE, 12, 24*.

These ideas are a strange mixture of profound and absurd. Tolstoy was deeply right in affirming the primacy of true religious, moral, and social thinking. The point is perennially valid, and especially salutary now that the achievements of natural science have become even more dazzling. And Tolstoy's analysis of motives to research is still telling. But as to the claims of scientific philosophers to establish an ethic without using specifically ethical concepts, I cannot believe that they were as shallow as Tolstoy alleged; though the concepts of 'fuller activity' and 'length and breadth of life' were, indeed, never satisfactorily clarified by Spencer, who hovered uneasily between some variety of pure evolutionism, and some form of evolutionistic hedonism.[1] Tolstoy's violent reaction to ethical use of the idea of 'struggle for existence' springs from his religious outlook. How could human existence be essentially a struggle, if its whole point was universal love? For Tolstoy Haeckel's views contravened the basis of all morality: the principle that every human life is sacrosanct. Both thinkers run to wrong extremes. Human life is not 'essentially' a struggle; nor is its whole point universal love. This is nearer the truth; but intelligent universal decency is a better ideal than universal love. Nor is every human life sacrosanct; though each deserves profound respect. But Tolstoy is surely right in placing morality beyond experimental science? And he hits hard at those who claim they know from their own sense of values who is harmful to the species. Yet Tolstoy's view that this cannot be known would really involve even greater forbearance and greater anarchism than he realized. It would involve complete absence of moral judgments—even Tolstoy's—and correspondingly in-

[1] This point emerges clearly from the excellent treatment of Spencer's ethics by Henry Sidgwick, *Lectures on the Ethics of T. H. Green, Herbert Spencer, and J. Martineau*, London, 1902, 135–312.

creased licence of action—even on the part of oppressive governments.

As to practical science, it is perhaps hard to say whether it has brought more good than harm. Tolstoy clearly saw the evils science had brought, but in his general views he did not fairly acknowledge the benefits, even those he made use of—the improved transport and postal facilities, the typewriter used by his daughter Alexandra, or the dictaphone he came to like. Nor did he foresee possible future benefits, for instance, that the hydrogen bomb *might* save us from world wars; or that practical science might eventually help towards a decentralization of population. And he might well not have approved of the increased leisure agricultural and industrial mechanization could bring.

Tolstoy's views on *theoretical* natural science are simply absurd. Aristotle and Bacon were great teachers, and Comte not negligible. Tolstoy underrated knowledge for its own sake. Even if 'humanity' as a whole might not wish to know the velocity of light, part of 'humanity'—many scientists—might; and the knowledge might be worthwhile intrinsically, and for understanding the world—apart from the countless benefits it might ultimately provide. And it seems likely that Tolstoy's own health and even life at times depended on certain medical practitioners having absorbed some of such 'useless' pieces of knowledge.

ON ART

Art is not a pleasure, a solace, or an amusement; art is a great matter.

Tolstoy, *What is Art?*

Tolstoy made several attempts to expound a theory of art based on his religious attitude, but the most

important is *What is Art?*,[1] written in 1898, long
after his conversion.

The question seemed to him vital, because of the
vast wealth and energy, including much unwilling
labour, then lavished on so-called 'art', and because
of other evils which it caused, such as over-special-
ization. Only genuine 'art' was nevertheless worthwhile.

Tolstoy dismisses beauty theories of art. 'Beauty'
had never been satisfactorily defined. The only
plausible account involved saying it was what hap-
pened to please a certain group. But this was like
saying the purpose of food was pleasure. Furthermore, the group to be pleased was in modern times
always taken as upper-class.

Tolstoy considers other theories: that art is (1) an
activity springing from 'sexual feeling and the pro-
pensity to play' (Schiller, Darwin, Spencer); (2) the
manifestation, in lines, colours, movements, sounds,
or words, of human emotions (Véron); (3) the pro-
duction of some permanent object or passing action
fitted not only to supply an active enjoyment to the
producer, but to convey a pleasurable impression to
spectators or listeners, apart from any personal
advantage they might gain (Sully). Tolstoy prefers
these to beauty-theories, but criticizes (1) as only an
account of the *origin* of art, (2) because art must act
on other people, (3) because it would include con-
juring-tricks and other activities which are not art,
and because many things which cause no pleasure to
producer or experiencer may be art.

Tolstoy's own definition, which clearly owes much
to Véron's, and something to Sully's, is this:

'Art is a human activity consisting in this, that
one man consciously by means of certain external
signs, hands on to others feelings he has lived

[1] *CE, 18.*

37

through, and that others are infected by those
feelings and also experience them.'

Art thus unites people in the same feelings, and so
is exceedingly important for humanity.

Tolstoy's 'infallible criterion' of genuine art is
infectiousness, and the stronger the infection the better
the art, 'as art'—'that is, not considering the value of
the feelings it transmits'. Degree of infectiousness
depended on three factors: (1) the individuality of
the feeling; (2) the clearness of its transmission; (3)
(above all) the sincerity of the artist, that is, the force
with which he felt the feeling.

The overall value of a work also depended on the
value of the feelings transmitted. Now, as we have
seen, Tolstoy thought humanity was continually
advancing towards perfection. Art's function was
to replace less kind and beneficial feelings by feelings
more necessary to human well-being. Which feelings
were more necessary was decided by the religious
consciousness of every age. The Greeks valued
feelings of beauty, strength and courage, and the art
transmitting them (e.g. Hesiod, Homer, Phidias);
and condemned crude sensuality, despondency and
effeminacy, and the art transmitting them. The Jews
approved feelings of devotion and submission to the
God of the Hebrews, and condemned feelings of
idolatry, and the art transmitting them (e.g. The
Golden Calf). The religious consciousness of contemporary Europe was *true* Christianity, 'the consciousness that our well-being both material and
spiritual, individual and collective, temporal and
eternal, lies in the growth of brotherhood among
men'. All art united some people. True Christian
art united all. But only two kinds of feeling would
do this: (1) feelings flowing from a consciousness of
our sonship to God and of the brotherhood of man,
such as humility, purity, compassion, love, and horror at the violation of love; (2) simple feelings of

common life accessible to everyone, e.g. merriment, pity, cheerfulness, tranquillity. Modern art, then, should transmit such feelings. Tolstoy gives as examples of literary art transmitting (1) ('Religious art'): *Die Räuber, Les Pauvres Gens* and *Les Misérables, A Tale of Two Cities, The Christmas Carol,* and other novels and tales of Dickens, *Adam Bede,* and the novels of Dostoyevski, especially his *Memoirs from the House of Death.* As possible examples of art transmitting (2) ('Universal art') he gives: *Don Quixote,* Molière's comedies, *David Copperfield, The Pickwick Papers,* the tales of Gogol and Pushkin, and some of the works of Maupassant; but thought none comparable with ancient universal art, such as the story of Joseph. He condemned all his own literary work to date, save the stories *God Sees the Truth but Waits* and *A Prisoner in the Caucasus,* candidates for Classes (1) and (2) respectively.[1]

All other art was bad in the feeling transmitted, for instance literary works transmitting ecclesiastical or patriotic feelings, and feelings exclusive to the idle rich, e.g. aristocratic honour, satiety, spleen, pessimism, and refined and vicious feelings flowing from sex-love. Shakespeare was objectionable because he pandered to the values of the ruling classes of his time, as well as because his characters were often unconvincing and his expression of feeling often unnatural.[2] Most modern art transmitted bad feelings, and so was worse than no art at all.

[1] Both tales are included in *Twenty-three Tales* in *CE, 13,* reprd. World's Classics.
[2] Tolstoy's essay *Shakespeare and the Drama* (1906) is translated in *CE, 21.* Tolstoy's views gave rise to a most interesting series of letters from Bernard Shaw to Tolstoy's disciple, Chertkov, who showed an English version to Shaw before publication. A short account of these is given by Professor Simmons (*Leo Tolstoy,* London, 1949, 689–91). For a longer account see S. Breitburg, 'B. Shaw v spore c Tolstym o Shekspire', *Literaturnoye Nasledstvo,* 37–38, Moscow, 1939, 617–32. See also for Tolstoy's whole attitude to Shakespeare, G. Gibian, *Tolstoj and Shakespeare,* s-Gravenhage, 1957.

But there was a remedy: to acknowledge Christ's real teaching, and encourage art which flowed from it. The art of the future would then be available and intelligible to all. It would be clear, simple and brief, and produced not by professional artists for gain or vanity, but by anyone living a normal working life, who had some special artistic talent to express worthwhile feelings he felt, as and when they arose. The task of art was immense. Through its influence, aided by true science, and guided by religion, the peaceful co-operation of men, now maintained externally, e.g. by law courts, police, charitable institutions, factory-inspection, could be attained by free, joyful activity, so that the reign of violence might come to an end.

These views command respect for their sincerity and thoughtfulness, and the high moral standard they set for art. But they are open to two kinds of criticism: challenges to Tolstoy's root scheme of values, such as we have already briefly made; and logico-philosophical objections, such as now follow.

Past failure to define beauty does not invalidate beauty-theories, for a good definition might yet be found, or beauty might be indefinable. Again, a slight amendment—that beauty gives particular kinds of *satisfaction*—would circumvent Tolstoy's food analogy. Thirdly, a definition of art in terms of feeling would not exclude a definition in terms of beauty or pleasure. Moreover, is it impossible that a group of people should exist who are only pleased by works which deserve to please, and could not 'art' be just what would please that group? Fourthly, Tolstoy's definition is defective, both because it makes the category of 'art' depend on *actual* rather than *appropriate* reactions, and because it involves the doubtful assertion that the artist has always felt the same feelings as his work stimulates. *Stimulation* would be a better concept than *infection*. Fifthly, Tolstoy's three factors affecting the degree of infectiousness, though of great interest, are unconvincing. Work expressing highly individual feeling may arouse resistance and fail to 'infect'. Again, 'clearness of transmission' is ambiguous. Tolstoy himself refuses to regard as 'clear' what would not be clear to an unsophisticated peasant, and yet admits that obscurely allusive work might be 'clearer' to those 'in the know' than unallusive work. In any case, surely a difficult work can infect as strongly and be as valuable as a work obvious to all? As to degree of sincerity, Tolstoy does not make it clear whether sincerity involves feelings of the artist *during creation*, and, in any case, it is at least doubtful whether strength of response varies with the strength of the artist's feelings either before or during creation. Sixthly, the sensations and thoughts stimulated by art seem sometimes just as important as its emotional content, and Tolstoy's concentration on emotion seems, therefore, to be unduly narrow. Further, in his historical account of the evaluation of 'feelings', Tolstoy seems often to speak of what would be more appropriately designated 'attitudes'.

Two final objections: First, Tolstoy sets such store by the value of the feelings communicated that finally he loses sight even of infectiousness, and denies value to his own most powerful work. Secondly, he seems unaware that degree of infectiousness depends not on the work alone but on the degree of resistance of its public, so that a fine and powerful work might not infect, and if so, according to Tolstoy's own criteria, it would not be a work of art at all.

He felt himself alive and young again.
Tolstoy on Prince Andrei after his waltz with Natasha.

He regards woman with the implacable animosity of
the male who has not derived from her all the pleasure
he had hoped,—or is it the hostility of the mind towards
the degrading impulses of the flesh?
Gorki, *Reminiscences of Tolstoy* (1901).

It is a striking fact that there is no substantial
appreciative portrait of a woman in any of the fiction
Tolstoy wrote between 1877 and his death in 1910.

The causes of this and of the bitter strictures Tolstoy passed on women in his late years are fairly
clear (see Ch. III). The point to be made at present is
that it was only after Tolstoy's conversion, and indeed some time after it (*c.* 1887), that he began to
express with considerable frequency in his diary and
elsewhere (e.g. in *The Kreutzer Sonata*) virulent views
on women. Even then really bitter remarks did not
predominate, save during his last few years. But he
gave the bitter remarks some appearance of system,
and it is interesting to consider them in relation to
his religious principles.

In *What I Believe* (1884) Tolstoy casts no slur on
women, love, or marriage. He even deduces the
doctrine of strict monogamy from the Sermon on the
Mount. Yet already in *The Gospel Teaching* (1881–3)
he had emphasized that Christ taught that the family
must not interfere with the life of the spirit. Not long
after, he began to find that the claims of his own family
did so interfere. In *On Life* (1881) he insists that love
is a reasonable kindly activity directed towards who-
ever happens to need it at the moment, and that it is
not that preference for one's wife or family, which is
conceived in man's 'animal personality', and often
overwhelms all other feelings.

In *The Kreutzer Sonata* (begun 1887; publ. 1889)

Tolstoy goes further, and maintains, with acrid violence, that the true Christian ideal is complete chastity, and that a Christian marriage is therefore impossible, though a married Christian may adopt a Christian attitude towards his marriage by making chastity his aim.[1] Tolstoy appealed to Christ's words in Matthew xix: 'There are eunuchs, which made themselves eunuchs for the kingdom of heaven's sake', but the support is clearly flimsy. In his *Postscript to the Kreutzer Sonata* he suggests that marriage itself is no less egoistic than sexual love, and thus incompatible with Christianity—a better attempt at justification, though probably invalid.

One further point before passing to criticism: since long before his conversion Tolstoy had been a convinced anti-feminist. He had thought that women could only really fulfil themselves in marriage, and that feminists were women who wished to escape their true responsibilities, and enjoy life without really deserving to. Curiously enough, even after Tolstoy came to reject marriage as anti-Christian, he still clung to his anti-feminism.

The views on women, love, and marriage developed by Tolstoy in and after 1887 are pernicious. It is absurd to think of women as tools of the devil. They are no worse than men. Some may thwart the ideals and achievements of their husbands, but many do not; and Tolstoy himself had cause to be grateful to his wife for the productive early years of his marriage. But he had come to believe in the dangerous idea that there is a fixed stock of welfare,

---

[1] The distinguished Soviet scholar and critic, Professor N. K. Gudzy, interestingly draws attention to the fact that these views only came into later drafts of *The Kreutzer Sonata*, after Tolstoy had corresponded extensively on sex and women with his wife's arch-enemy, V. G. Chertkov. (N. K. Gudzy, *Kak rabotal Tolstoy*, Moscow, 1936, 37–69: and see also Jubilee Edition, Vol. 27, 563–610.)

withdrawal from which for self, wife, or family, means less for others. He failed to see that exertions grounded in reasonable, and even in unreasonable, egoism, may increase the stock inconceivably. He also failed to see that the spark and fire of sexual love might have equal claims to divinity with the rational feeling of universal kindliness. And he failed to see that the best way of fostering universal benevolence might be to satisfy individual love rather than to suppress it.

Again, as was at once pointed out to Tolstoy, complete chastity for all would involve extermination of the human race. His reply was that complete chastity was 'only an ideal'. It might be an ideal for those whose aims were possibly incompatible with love for wife and family, but it is hard to see why it should even be 'an ideal' for all. To condemn every deviation from chastity, even within marriage, is not only silly but a blasphemy against life.

In *The Kreutzer Sonata*, Tolstoy, through Pozdnyshev, complains that women have been brought up from childhood to please men so that they can capture a man and marry him. Some do it by music and curls, others by learning and political services, says Pozdnyshev, in a passage suppressed by the censor.[1] This is very like Schopenhauer's *Essay on Women*. Both Schopenhauer and Tolstoy regard this general practice as most reprehensible, instead of simply advising men to be on their guard to protect important aims, and avoid taking the wrong mate. But both Schopenhauer and Tolstoy also regard the practice as a civilized form of an overpowering *natural* instinct; and their negative reactions are therefore nihilistic. If they had considered the practice *unnatural* they could have been expected to suggest remedies for it which would restore the 'natural' order; but neither of them could seriously maintain that it was not 'natural' for women to attract men.

[1] See World's Classics edn., 542.

44

They were therefore forced to adopt the nihilistic course of attacking the natural order itself.

Tolstoy had often had healthier ideas on women, love, and marriage, before 1887, and these are expressed and implied in some of the earlier stories and the two great novels. There we find him understanding and valuing the true love of men for women, and women for men, and their division of responsibilities within the marriages which at least seem to be the right destiny for most human beings.

II

The Pages of Fiction

> At the basis of a true work of art there must lie some
> perfectly original idea or feeling, but it must be
> expressed with slavish adherence to the smallest details
> of life.
>
> Tolstoy, to A. B. Goldenweizer (1907).

Tolstoy's writings fall into three fairly distinct
periods: 1851–autumn 1863, the period before he
began *War and Peace*; 1863–77, the period of *War
and Peace* and *Anna Karenina*; and 1878–1910, the
period after Tolstoy's conversion. Let us look at
some of the fiction of each of the three periods in
turn, and then briefly consider its evolution and
character.

1851–Autumn 1863

Tolstoy always thought that a work of art must be
deeply personal and original, and scrupulously faithful to life. But he was also, from the first, concerned
with literary texture and form.

When Tolstoy's literary career seriously began he
drew at once on personal experiences. The curious
fragment, *A Story of Yesterday*,[1] his most ambitious
attempt before *Childhood*, offers a minute record of
his experiences of twenty-four hours. It was, however, no mere transcription of life, but a highly
self-conscious re-arrangement and amplification of
a number of Tolstoy's diary entries, stretching over
many days. The work is lively, and vividly displays
two features typical of Tolstoy's work—the extended
internal monologue and the portrayal of mental
events and characteristics through their physical

[1] Publ. in Jubilee Edn. (hereafter referred to as *JE*), *1*,
279–95.

manifestations. Tolstoy abandoned it, however, to create a work of art out of a remoter period of his life.

Childhood, Tolstoy's first published work, is an attempt to recapture the distilled essence of childhood through a series of distinct episodes recounted so as to bring to life not only the scenes and situations, but the feelings experienced, and especially those of the child-'hero', Nikolenka. The work is not only vital but elegant. The primary literary influence was Sterne's *Sentimental Journey*, and we find, indeed, the *Journey's* spare selectiveness,[1] momentary intensity and limpid style, but *Childhood* has more genuine warmth, greater moral seriousness, more depth and variety of feeling, and rather less whimsicality.[2] Tolstoy himself, in his Preface, asks his reader to read the tale 'looking for the parts that grip your heart, and not for such as make you laugh'. Yet without the comic passages the grip on our hearts would be perceptibly loosened. Tolstoy's attempt to deflect the reader's attention from the gratuitous humour of which he had a strong vein is noteworthy, especially as we find him also during this early phase naming humour as one of his criteria of literary value. Even in *Childhood*, however, serious intentions and the urge to fun are sometimes reconciled by yoking humour for satiric purposes—a procedure

---

[1] It has been pointed out by the Soviet critic P. S. Popov, in an article in *Literaturnoye Nasledstvo, 35–6*, Moscow, 1939, that in the whole of *Childhood* only two days of living are actually described. (Popov's article also analyses the extent of the influence on *Childhood* of Töpffer, Dickens and Rousseau.)

[2] N. N. Gusev (in *L. N. Tolstoy, Materialy k biographii, 1828–55*, Moscow, 1954) has rightly drawn attention to the fact that the first draft was written in a much less serious tone; but that already in the second draft sincerity and depth of feeling had become predominant. Attention has also been drawn to evidence both in Tolstoy's diaries and in successive drafts of the work, that he was trying to force himself to break free from Sterne's habits of digression (see B. Eykhenbaum, *Molodoy Tolstoy*, Petrograd, 1922, and P. S. Popov, *art. cit.*).

more fully exploited in *Sevastopol in May*, fairly frequent in *War and Peace* and *Anna Karenina*, and very common in work of the last period. Yet, at first, satire itself was not wholly acceptable to Tolstoy, and we find diary entries expressing his reluctance to use the powerful satiric gift which he could not suppress.[1]

A salient feature of *Childhood* is the thoroughgoing watchfulness of the analysis of Nikolenka's emotional reactions. This is particularly striking in episodes where these reactions were unusually powerful, as in the vivid scene of the holy fool Grisha praying to God in the attic allotted to him on one of his visits to the great house, while the children huddle together in the dark, listening, and watching him as he stands out clearly in the moonlight. Tolstoy emphasizes the unforgettably moving impression Grisha's confession of sins made on Nikolenka, and amplifies its religious significance; but having done so he inexorably records the fading of the child's emotion, because his curiosity was satisfied, his legs were stiff, and he wanted to join in the whispering and romping of the other children. This is an early instance of the union of immense feeling with unsentimental honesty so frequent in Tolstoy's writing. Whether he *was* rigorously honest in such passages is irrelevant. In literature it is the impression of honesty that counts, not honesty itself.

Childhood is a harbinger of Tolstoy's mature fiction in other ways also. The theme of death, which was to haunt him later, is already present, and, indeed, has the last word. And an attitude which was perhaps lifelong in Tolstoy is expressed in the brief sentence about the death of the housekeeper, Natalya Savishna:

> She achieved the best and greatest thing in life— she died without regrets and without fear.

[1] E.g. *Diary*, 1 and 3 Dec. 1852.

The animal excitement of the hunting scene is a fore-taste of the great chapters of *War and Peace*. The anxieties and absurdities of Nikolenka make the child the father of Pierre. *Childhood* also has many of the formal features which were to become typical. There is the abrupt beginning. There are the short chapters. There are the digressions, in which Tolstoy expresses, through his protagonist, his opinions on life, people, and art. These features again partly derive from Sterne. There are also, however, some of the very opinions (for instance, the intense dislike of hypocrisy, and the mistrust and contempt for artificial writing [1]), which will run through Tolstoy's whole career.

But *Childhood* is not merely a precursor of Tolstoy's mature work, it is fine in its own right—chiefly perhaps in virtue of its controlled lyrical nostalgia, its moral power, the brilliant choice of scenes, the economy of the writing, the vivid impact of the characters, and the sure touch shown in the psychology of childhood.

Tolstoy soon began to think of *Childhood* as the first part of a large novel on the 'Four Epochs' of his life to date, childhood, boyhood, youth, and early manhood.[2] He seems to have wanted to trace his own growth and work it into art, to comment on his changing environment, and to show the weakness of an intelligent and sensitive person in face of his growing egoism and vanity, and of the influences of artificial education and worldly society.[3]

Tolstoy never wrote the fourth part of this novel. *Boyhood* and *Youth*, the second and third parts, are less

---

[1] In his observations on the superiority of 'nature' to 'art' Tolstoy approaches the realistic aesthetic of Belinski and Chernyshevski.

[2] This expansive planning was typical of Tolstoy both as man and as writer. Among his fiction, *A Landowner's Morning*, *The Cossacks*, *War and Peace* and *Resurrection* are all cases of works which were only part of some greater unrealized project.

[3] See *Diary*, 30 Nov. 1852.

remarkable than *Childhood*, though they maintain its general structure—a series of set scenes with little attempt to mould them into a continuous narrative. The scenes are generally less striking, though in *Boyhood* the storm scene is wonderfully perceptive, and the history lesson a sheer delight, while in *Youth* the hero's awkward behaviour in society, and his confused sensations about young women, as well as the episodes of the University examinations and their aftermath, offer splendid instances of the self-critically ironical humour which so often forms an element in Tolstoy's 'dialectic of the soul'.

While he was writing of these earlier experiences, Tolstoy was living a life of a very different kind—the Army life of the Caucasus and later of the Crimean War. Besides giving perspective and sometimes irony to Tolstoy's view of his past, this formed the stuff of some new works of fiction.

Several of these—for instance, *The Raid, Recollections of a Billiard Marker*, the Sevastopol Sketches, and *The Wood-felling*—were thrown into the press, but the best of them, *The Cossacks*, was nursed and rounded into one of Tolstoy's very finest works.[1] Much of the other work, however, has three signal features, its fresh, powerful, and often stern impressions of the details of campaigning life, its scathing satire on the glory of war as such,[2] and its depreciation of the vain showy soldier in comparison with the quiet man who accepts emergencies and does his duty without any eye to reward.

The Sevastopol Sketches have a place apart, not only because they were written from first-hand experience of an event of major importance, but because of the strong and somewhat conflicting feelings

[1] Though Tolstoy himself intended to work further at it, and only published it (in 1863) to pay a debt at cards.

[2] *Sevastopol in December 1854* does, however, glorify the defenders of the city, just as *War and Peace* glorifies the defenders of Russia.

expressed in them. *Sevastopol in December 1854* is a glorification of the defenders, but in *Sevastopol in May 1855* we find bitter condemnations of war and exposure of the meanness and egoism of many of the participants. This is continued in *Sevastopol in August 1855*, yet here patriotism fires Tolstoy again, and he is stung with shame and indignation at the Russian defeat. A similar conflict of feelings appears in *Anna Karenina*, about the Serbo-Turkish war.

The Cossacks is somewhat complex in conception. The story of Olenin, disillusioned at twenty-four with the empty card-playing existence of a young man about Moscow, travelling to the Caucasus in search of a new life, settling for a time on a Cossack *stanitsa*,[1] falling in love with a beautiful Cossack girl, who turns him down for a young Cossack brave, is used by Tolstoy for some large-scale polemic purposes. First, though subordinately, he deflates romanticized conceptions of life in the Caucasus, such as those retailed by Lermontov [2] and Bestuzhev-Marlinsky.[3] Though he portrays the warlike side of Cossack life, he also emphasizes the peaceful occupations of the Cossacks, their cultivation of vines and fruit trees, maize, millet, melons, and pumpkins, and their fishing and hunting. Secondly, and dominantly, Tolstoy is concerned to contrast the productiveness and moral worth of Cossack life with the aimless wastefulness of the *jeunesse dorée* of Moscow. Even the operations of war seem to him justified, as defence

[1] A Cossack village settlement.
[2] Lermontov's *A Hero of Our Times*, itself a disillusioned rather than romanticized work, was published in 1840; but he had also written an unfinished romance of the Pugachov Rebellion; and both his early verse tale *Hajji Abrek* and the mature poems *The Demon* and *Mtsyri* are full of somewhat lurid Caucasian impressions.
[3] Bestuzhev (1797–1837), a Decembrist who, on release from Siberia, served in the ranks in the Caucasus, and wrote novels under the name of A. Marlinsky. The best-known is *Ammalet Bek* (1832), a story of the Caucasian war.

of the Russian frontiers against Moslem marauding or invasion. The main Cossack characters, old Yeroshka, young Lukashka, and the splendid and strong girl Maryana, are all shown as full of health, vitality, and moral dignity. Again, while refusing to indulge in false lyricism, Tolstoy finds poetic inspiration in these characters and the Cossack way of life, and in the beauty of the Caucasian mountains. Many of the impressions come to us through the mind of Olenin, who also represents the passionate searches for a morally satisfying attitude to life which we find in Tolstoy's diaries of 1851–4. Much as Olenin loves the Cossack life, however, he is unable to assimilate himself to it, and his rupture with Maryana and subsequent departure are told of with insight and bleak frankness. The elements could not mix; and this is yet another criticism of Olenin's background. Olenin is more struck by the Cossacks than they are by him. Especially fascinating for him is Daddy Yeroshka, the enormous old hunter, with the deep bass voice, and tremendous zest for life, action, story-telling, and joking, and the belief that at the end 'the grass grows over you, and that's all'. Yeroshka's courage is companioned by the sense that all this killing of Chechens and Cossacks, who ought to live at peace, is a very foolish business. In his talks with Olenin he gives his solutions to some of Olenin's (and Tolstoy's) deepest questions about existence; and the solutions spring from an unfailing vitality which neither Olenin nor Tolstoy had in that measure. Yeroshka is the symbol for the early Tolstoy of that same life-force whose claims we shall see strangely reasserted nearly half-a-century later in *Hadji Murad*.

The Cossacks (with *Childhood*) stands supreme among the work of Tolstoy's first period. Its vivid presentation of external and internal life, its combined use of objective description, spoken language, and psychological presentation, and the clarity and forceful expression of the ultimate guiding ideas, are probably unrivalled in Tolstoy.

One short work on which Tolstoy was also engaged during those Army years stands apart both from the stories of recollection and from those of campaigning life. This is *A Landowner's Morning*, in which Tolstoy gives expression to the heart-searchings and problems of a young landowner who wishes to do the best by his peasants. This is a fragment of a large novel, *The Novel of a Russian Landowner*, which Tolstoy had planned in 1852, and which was intended to be dogmatic and instructive. The story presents the main problem well, but makes it seem like an impasse, and it may well be that Tolstoy abandoned the large work because he could not find any solution which satisfied him.

Two Hussars, *Lucerne*, and *Family Happiness* belong to the period after Tolstoy's return from Sevastopol in November 1856 and before his decision late in 1859 to found a school at Yasnaya Polyana. *Two Hussars*, originally called *Father and Son*, is the story of two brief amatory episodes in a provincial town. The first involves the father, the second, some decades later, the son. The guiding idea is to contrast the bold openness and full-bodied romanticism of an earlier and better epoch, with the cynical egoism, meanness, and timidity of life in the mid-century. In this respect we have a foretaste of *War and Peace*. *Lucerne* is one of the products of Tolstoy's first journey abroad. It is a short, indignant protest at the inhumanity of the elegant tourists, staying at the Schweizerhof Hotel, who listened enthralled to an itinerant guitarist, but did not throw a single copper when the music was over. This burning and moving work is the expression of Tolstoy's disgust at the moral weakness of Western European 'civilization'. (It should perhaps be added, however, that Tolstoy was equally disgusted, on his return to Russia, with the barbaric beatings, thieving and lawlessness he encountered there.) After the failure of his story of a dipsomaniac musician, *Albert* (publ. 1858), Tolstoy came out both against professional writing and against art which concerned itself with contemporary social and political questions, instead of matters of universal import. It was during this phase that he wrote *Family Happiness*, based on his relations with Valerya Arseneva, a girl he had nearly married about two years before.[1] In the story the hero and heroine actually marry, and there is much friction owing to their difference of age and outlook, though eventually both friction and passion cease, and they settle down to a peaceful and contented existence. The story also brings out the threat to family happiness and genuine human values, from worldly life in high society. *Family Happiness* is a fine work, generally underrated even now, but cold-shouldered with gross injustice at the time by those critics who were concerned to maintain the socio-political elements in fiction. There is throughout the work a delicate touch for concrete detail both physical and psychological, and a firm grasp of the main theme, which is made extremely convincing. As a result of the ill-success of *Family Happiness* with critics and public, Tolstoy was discouraged, and decided to give up writing fiction. He started his school at Yasnaya Polyana. His renewed contact with the peasants, however, soon made him think of writing peasant stories. This idea bore real fruit during his second journey to Western Europe to study educational methods. Tolstoy started *Polikushka* in Brussels in March 1861, and it was published two years later. *Polikushka* is a heartrending tale of a rather incompetent serf who fervently wishes to please his owner, and is entrusted with an errand. He fails through a series of accidents, with the help of some drink, and, as a result, hangs himself. The blend of powerful

[1] The story is told by its heroine. Tolstoy took this idea from *Jane Eyre*.

54

feeling with robust and somewhat malicious humour in this story is a frequent one in Tolstoy. Here the humour is partly that of the peasants themselves, but it is so fully realized by Tolstoy, and his own humour is so similar, that one can understand the suggestion that, despite his aristocracy, he was basically himself a *muzhik*.[1]

So far Tolstoy had written almost entirely from personal experience. All his themes, moreover, were contemporary. Some had a social or political bearing. All had serious moral content. And Tolstoy had been persistently concerned to depict reality vividly and naturally, to give no quarter in self-analysis, and not to blink harsh realities, such as the horrors of war.

In much of this Tolstoy was simply following the general practice of the 'Realistic School' (*Naturalnaya Shkola*) which included writers as various as Herzen, Grigorovich, Turgenev, Dostoyevski, and Goncharov. Many diary entries between 1847 and 1857 show Tolstoy's admiration for writers of this 'School'.

Tolstoy's originality lay largely in his character and in his special experiences as child of the nobility, landowner, and soldier. By and large he simply worked superlatively well on this material within the bounds of an established tradition.

In some of the later work of this phase, however, he does try to push beyond the bounds of personal experience. In *Family Happiness*, for instance, he imaginatively extends suggestions from an episode in his own life into description of a married life he had not yet known; and he even tells the story from the woman's point of view. In *Polikushka* he brilliantly projects himself into the mind of the peasant.

[1] Tolstoy himself actually told Gorki that he was more of a *muzhik* than Gorki was.

In the work of the next phase we find the powers of introspection, observation, imaginative extension, and projection combined in large-scale achievements which express the broad and deep concerns of a rich and mature personality.

> The novel has tasks, even external tasks, the description of a whole human life or of many human lives, and thus anyone writing a novel must have a clear and firm attitude as to what is good and bad in life.
> Tolstoy, *On the Works of Maupassant*, 1894.

War and Peace changed character greatly during composition. It was first planned as a novel of aristocratic family affairs, set in the early years of the century. Contemporary events were to batter its characters; but they were to emerge purified and serene. It seems that Tolstoy was partly motivated by a desire to write about members of his own family whom he loved or admired, and other persons whom he detested; and partly by a wish to oppose to the beliefs and behaviour of the rising bourgeoisie of the 'sixties the ideals of the best of the old aristocratic families, their culture, and their contribution to the life of Russia. Then Tolstoy telescoped this plan with another conceived as early as 1856: to write a novel round an exiled hero of the Decembrist Revolt of 1825. In 1863 he thought first of setting the novel in 1856, the date of the Decembrist hero's return from Siberia; then changed plan, and thought of 1825 as the starting point; then 1812, the year of the Napoleonic invasion, then 1808, then 1805. One surviving draft preface announces his intention to develop his characters among the historical events of 1805, 1807, 1812, and 1856. Eventually he limited himself substantially to 1805–14; but he never forgot the later years, and Pierre Bezukhov must always be thought of as Tolstoy's Decembrist. That is one leading theme. Tolstoy's historical research had, however, led him to another. In March 1865 a reading of the Memoirs of Marmont, one of Napoleon's marshals, swept him with the idea of writing 'a psychological history—a novel on Alexander and Napoleon. All the emptiness, verbiage, stupidity and contradictions of the people round them, and their own.'[1] Tolstoy wrote no such separate novel: the great idea stormed its way into *War and Peace*. This was early. Tolstoy had only covered the year 1805 before the new idea came to him. Soon after, we find him saying that he intended to depict the historical personalities in all their activities; but he draws back from this, and decides just to tell 'what it is indispensable to tell'. When Tolstoy came to write of 1812, his work gathered momentum, and in May 1866 he tells Fet that it should be ready in 1867 for publication, under the title *All's Well That Ends Well*. There exists in draft a plan of the rest of the novel, probably drawn up early in 1866.[2] There are marked differences from the novel as we know it. Platon Karatayev does not yet exist. Neither Petya Rostov nor Prince Andrei dies. The philosophy of history scarcely appears. But in reading of the war of 1812 Tolstoy had come across such works as F. N. Glinka's *Letters of a Russian Officer*[3] and Denis Davydov's *Diary*,[4] which emphasized the role of the people in the national struggle with Napoleon. Tolstoy was lifted into a wide sweep of speculation on the causes of the great

[1] *Diary*, 19 March 1865.

[2] See *JE*, *13*, 35-6.

[3] Glinka was a Decembrist who had taken part in the 1812 campaign. His *Letters* (*Pisma russkovo ofitsera*, Moscow, 1821) made a great stir at the time.

[4] Davydov had fought with partisan detachments in 1812, and in his *Diary* (*Dnevnik partizanskikh deistvi 1812 goda*) not only gives an account of the organization and methods of the partisans, but also advances views on the importance of the moral factors in war, which clearly influenced Tolstoy.

events of 1805 and 1812. Surely they could not have been caused by petty characters like Napoleon? And so we have Tolstoy's thoughts on causality in history, rooted in discussions with his Moscow friends, and in his reading of Proudhon's *La Guerre et la paix*, Joseph de Maistre's *Correspondance diplomatique* and *Soirées de St. Petersbourg* and the *Historical Aphorisms* of Pogodin.[1] Tolstoy works over all he has written, changes the title to *War and Peace*, and continues writing. The novel is now geared to the conception of fatalism, under Divine Providence, and to the belief in the dominant role of the people in the war of 1812. Three volumes of *War and Peace* come out in 1867, the fourth in 1868, and the last two in 1869.

War and Peace is a resounding success as a hymn of glory to the great and triumphant effort of the Russian people in 1812. It is, however, no less successful as a satire on the failures of 1805. Tolstoy tells us that he went back to 1805 because he felt he could not properly tell the story of triumph without first telling the story of shame. His account of both probably owed its ultimate drive to his experience of the loss of Sevastopol despite its heroic defence. He had sensed the corruption and incompetence that lay behind that defeat, and had had living contact with the splendid efforts of the actual defenders. 1862, the year before Tolstoy began his novel, was the fiftieth anniversary of the glories of 1812, and would naturally have suggested to him, as it did to other writers, such as Dobrolyubov, a comparison between the Crimean *débâcle* and that great time. It is also understandable that Tolstoy should have gone back to the failures of 1805. It took him some time, however, to arrive at the

[1] For the influence of these writers on *War and Peace* see B. Eykhenbaum—*Lev Tolstoy*, Vol. I. Leningrad, 1928, Vol. II, Moscow, 1931; N. Brian-Chaninov, *La Guerre et la Paix de Léon Tolstoï*, Paris, 1931; and I. Berlin, *The Hedgehog and the Fox*, London, 1953. M. P. Pogodin (1800–75) was Professor of Russian History at Moscow University. Tolstoy knew him personally.

mature view expressed in the novel as we know it, of the causes of the muddles and defeats of 1805 and of the triumphs of 1812: namely, that the muddles and defeats stemmed largely from the vanity and egoism of official and higher military circles in both Austria and Russia, resulting in what were for Russia the aimless campaigns of 1805; and that the triumphs sprang from the patriotism, self-sacrifice, tenacity and courage of that great body of the Russian people, of all classes, who were not tarred with the corruptions of intrigue, but fired with a spirit of idealism. The war of 1805 had had no meaning: the war of 1812 had the meaning of life and death.

This view is, however, overlaid with the philosophy of fatalism resulting from Tolstoy's latest reflections on history. The upshot is a definite inconsistency in the book.

The germs of Tolstoy's fatalistic philosophy of history probably lay in his hatred of Napoleon and all he stood for. Napoleon was for him an upstart, parasite, and bluffer, blown out with conceit. Such a person could not really sway the destinies of nations, he could only imagine he did. Tolstoy tries to deflate Napoleon by the philosophical generalization that the higher a person stands in the political hierarchy the less are his freedom and influence. Against him Tolstoy sets Kutuzov, beloved of his men, unpretentious, on the whole (though Tolstoy's characterization is somewhat inconsistent) passive, allowing events to take their course, because he knows that he cannot really influence them. By setting Kutuzov against Napoleon, Tolstoy was also dissenting from official historiography, which made Alexander I the saviour of Russia. For Tolstoy, Alexander could not make a satisfactory counter-figure. He was too vain himself. Tolstoy, though true to his values, and expressing them with great power (despite the inconsistencies), is unfair both to Napoleon and to Kutuzov. Anyone who has read Napoleon's own letters, or the accounts of Ségur [1] or of Tolstoy's own favourite, Stendhal, [2] or even of the critical Bourrienne, [3] knows there was more to Napoleon than appears in Tolstoy's ear-pinching, eau-de-cologne-spraying caricature. Tolstoy's Napoleon, though, had to be the epitome of the empty vanity of military and political ambition. For the author of the second and third Sevastopol sketches, master-stripper of snobbery and sham, the Emperor was prime material. The result is preposterous; but it has the power of Aristophanes. Tolstoy was actually well back in the queue of debunkers of Napoleon, [4] though he had long ago been impressed with the pettiness of the Napoleon of St. Helena, as he appeared in Las Cases [5] and O'Meara. [6] The portrait in *War and Peace*, however, though grossly one-sided, has probably become the classic of negative accounts. In the flush of his philosophy of history, Tolstoy also misrepresented Kutuzov. He failed to do justice to his intelligent generalship. There is documentary evidence that a number of the Russian successes which Tolstoy ascribed to collective action or even to waiting on providence, were in fact planned by Kutuzov, and achieved on his orders. [7] But Tolstoy's latest

[1] Ph. de Ségur, *Mémoires d'un aide-de-camp de Napoléon I*, Paris, 1824.

[2] Stendhal, *Vie de Napoléon*, 1837.

[3] L. A. F. de Bourrienne, *Mémoires sur Napoléon*, Paris, 1828–30.

[4] The head of the queue was probably British and American (Scott and Channing), and then came French, Belgian and Swiss historians.

[5] D. de Las Cases, *Mémorial de Ste.-Hélène*, Paris, 1823–4.

[6] B. E. O'Meara, *Napoleon in Exile, or A Voice from St. Helena*, London, 1822.

[7] See S. P. Bychkov, *L. N. Tolstoy*, Moscow, 1954, which quotes (p. 209) extracts from Kutuzov's orders, reprinted in *Znamya*, 1948 (No. 5), and also draws attention (p. 207) to Stalin's pronouncement in *Bolshevik*, 1941 (No. 3) that Kutuzov 'destroyed Napoleon and his army with the help of well-planned counter-attacks'—which, in view of the documentary evidence, seems to have been more than mere propaganda.

conception of the man did not merely require that Kutuzov should be modest and at one with the people. It required that nothing outstandingly positive should be due to generalship, and that the greatness of the Russian leader should lie in his sense of his own impotence and in his faith in Divine Providence. In point of fact, this cut across Tolstoy's earlier conception of Kutuzov, which survives in the scenes with Bennigsen, and in the energy of the outburst against Barclay de Tolly.

Tolstoy's philosophy of history was also a weapon against intellectualism, in the sense of the belief that human understanding can control future events. Tolstoy shows aversion to such confidence elsewhere.[1] In *War and Peace* the aversion appears largely in his satire on the pedantry of the generals of German origin; but also in Andrei's disillusion with the narrowly intellectual character of Speranksy. Here again Tolstoy falls into an unwarrantable extreme. Human understanding has *some* control over future events. Because events sometimes catch out human forethought it by no means follows that forethought should not be exercised. Nor does it follow that a general has no more influence on the course of a battle than any single private soldier. Tolstoy's philosophy of history is, however, not merely untrue, it involves him in general inconsistency. There is not space here to argue this in detail; but, to take one instance, Tolstoy wishes both to heap blame on Napoleon for the great suffering he caused in Europe, and to belittle him as a person who did not realize that everything he did was due to chance.

The philosophy of history is, however, very much part of the total impression of the novel; and it accords to some degree with religious attitudes expressed by characters in the non-theoretical sections;

[1] E.g. in the *ABC*, in *Anna Karenina*, in *On Life*, and in scattered references to science; also in the article *On Socialism* written just before he died (tr. L. Perno, London, 1936).

for instance, with the belief in Divine Providence so fervently held by Princess Marya, and by Platon Karatayev. Karatayev, on the other hand, is himself inconsistent with the spirit of resistance shown by the general run of the soldiers and peasants. Critics sometimes reproach Tolstoy for creating in Karatayev a character lacking in individuality.[1] That is beside the point. Karatayev is for Tolstoy a symbol of the best in the Russian peasantry, together with the still better which it might become. He represents many of the ideals which Tolstoy upheld later. Yet in *War and Peace* he is somewhat anomalous in his meek spirit of non-resistance, though not wholly so, since his good-heartedness, sincerity, and spirit of self-sacrifice are to a large degree shared by the best of the leading characters, by Pierre, by Natasha, and, in course of time, by Andrei.

One of the great features of *War and Peace*, indeed, is its moral strength. This comes out partly in the masterly description of the stream of consciousness, and the psychological and moral evolution of these leading characters. Tolstoy succeeds in giving us the most intimate sense of their moment-to-moment thoughts and feelings, while retaining critical distance from them, as when he brings out the somewhat ridiculous and amateurish role of Pierre,[2] and the harsh dryness which at times comes over Andrei. He sees the woeful incompleteness of Andrei's cynical attitude early in the novel; he sees Pierre quite clearly as on the brink of moral destruction after his disillusion with Freemasonry and his adherence to the Chamberlains' Club; and he sees Natasha's spon-

[1] E.g. D. S. Mirsky in his excellent *History of Russian Literature*, ed. 1949, 621.
[2] D. H. Lawrence called Bezukhov 'that porpoise of a Pierre'; and it is natural to wonder why both Pierre and Levin have something ridiculous about them. I think the answer is that Tolstoy was using a kind of irony—that he was too proud to put his moral aspirations into a character whose appeal would be obvious to convention-satisfied readers.

taneous love of life make her an easy though inno-
cent prey to the unscrupulous Anatole. Tolstoy
follows the moral evolution of each; and he cares for
it, and makes us care too. He makes us care more for
what is fine in human character. Both Pierre and
Andrei are brought to a religious attitude towards
moral issues; and to the sense that love and self-
sacrifice and forgiveness are supreme human values.
The moral strength of the work comes out also in
the contrasts drawn between these characters and
shallow worldlings, like the Kuragins, Anna Pav-
lovna Scherer, or careerists like Benningsen and the
up-and-coming Boris Droubetskoy. For here as
elsewhere, Tolstoy is a great satirist, as well as a
great enthusiast. The satire is sometimes sharp and
obvious; but sometimes works by implication, as in
the fact that in the decent old aristocratic family of the
Rostovs, in contrast to Anna Scherer's *salon*, French
is scarcely ever spoken. The values of closeness to
nature seem to be brought out almost instinctively by
Tolstoy, as in the scene at the 'little uncle's', where
Natasha dances a folk-dance with such fire and enthusiasm, or when she finds the opera artificial and
distasteful. Here we are not far from some of the
positions of *What is Art?* and, indeed, in *War and
Peace* there are plenty of foretastes of the values of the
later Tolstoy.

Yet *War and Peace* is, after all, a fuller affirmation of
life in all its plenitude than we find anywhere else in
Tolstoy. It is not wholly so, indeed. Some of the
last chapters which Tolstoy wrote convey a certain
sense of futility: the futility, for instance, of the
passage of great armies to and fro across the European continent. But too much of the novel had been
written for the gangrenous doubt to spread over it.
The overall impression is certainly that not merely
high moral values, but many kinds of human activities, including such things as Tolstoy was later to
condemn, like hunting, balls, parties, and so on, are

often worthwhile in themselves. There is even the sense that despite all the ghastly sufferings of·the war, which Tolstoy does not blink, it is possible and even right to face life cheerfully and without melancholy. The war itself is a glorious war, a war with a meaning; and that, for the later Tolstoy, is a contradiction. There is also in *War and Peace* that strong sense of the beauty and attraction of physical objects, as in Homer; which is a sign of a high level of vitality. This was present in the earlier work, and it is still present in some degree in *Anna Karenina*; but in the later work it only appears in a sustained form in *Hadji Murad*.

War and Peace is, however, not merely closer to the earlier than to the later work. It is to a considerable degree a further exploration of themes and kinds of experience which have already occurred in Tolstoy's fiction. The war episodes are an extension of the early military stories and sketches in a new and larger setting. The sense of nature, and life and death, and their fundamental questions, continue the trains already started in *Boyhood* and *Youth* and *The Cossacks*. The attempts by Pierre and Andrei to solve the problem of land reform carry on the themes raised in *A Landowner's Morning*. Even the insistence on the distinctive marks of the first· decade of the century had already been at least signposted in *Two Hussars*. The theme of the *Recollections of a Billiard Marker* is made classic in Nicholas Rostov's disastrous gambling venture. The poetry of the family life of the Rostovs harks back to *Childhood*, *Boyhood*, and *Youth*, and to *Family Happiness*, which itself points forward not only to the endorsement of the family in the Epilogue to *War and Peace*, but also to the fuller and more exclusive preoccupation with family life in *Anna Karenina*. It is not merely that in *War and Peace* we encounter many facets of life; it is that we find here reiterated and pushed further in one work a considerable number of what had been for some time Tolstoy's most vital concerns. Also, although many of the insistent questions and problems in some sense receive no solution, in another they do. The minds of the characters, no longer perplexed, cease to ask the questions. In *War and Peace* as we know it, Pierre finds ultimate satisfaction in family life and in working for his political ideals. Andrei indeed dies, but the experiences of the great love and the great war have left him 'purified and serene'. Yet the main purpose has been given to life by a national war. What other great purposes can give it a meaning? This is a question that will soon face Tolstoy more squarely than it has ever done before.

Tolstoy finished *War and Peace* in 1869. The subject of *Anna Karenina* occurred to him very soon after. On 24 February 1870 he mentioned to his wife the possibility of writing a novel whose theme would be that of a woman of the highest society ruining herself through a moral lapse. His task would be to make this woman seem only pitiful, not guilty. Tolstoy did not, however, even begin to work on such a book, and, indeed, the very next day he wrote the first sketch for a novel on the epoch of Peter the Great. This was in turn interrupted by a period during which he threw himself into the study of Greek, and by a subsequent nervous breakdown which may have been partly due to worry over the radical divergencies between Greek views of life and the Christian views in which he had been brought up.[1] Tolstoy's wife induced him to go to Samara for a *kumys*[2] cure. When he returned home in autumn 1871, he became absorbed in pedagogical work. He compiled his first *ABC Book*, intended as a complete educational curriculum for beginners; and he used it at Yasnaya

[1] Maude, *Life of Tolstoy*, World's Classics, I, 326, on the authority of the *Recollections* of S. A. Behrs, Tolstoy's brother-in-law.

[2] *Kumys* is fermented mare's-milk.

Polyana in classes for the peasant children of the district.[1] Then he turned again to the Peter the Great novel. He did considerable historical research for it throughout 1872 and the early months of 1873, but in March he laments to Strakhov and Fet that the novel is 'not moving'. Shortly afterwards, however, comes a surprise. Just after mid-March Sonya writes to her sister Tatyana Kuzminsky: 'Yesterday Lyovochka suddenly and unexpectedly began to write a novel of contemporary life. The subject of the novel —an unfaithful wife, and the whole drama following from that.' He finished a rough draft in less than two months, and hoped to finish the book the same year; but in the end it took him four years.

The story of the writing and publication of *Anna Karenina* is highly interesting, but too long to tell here in detail.[2] Certain salient points, however, bear strongly upon interpretation of the novel as we know it, and upon evaluation of Tolstoy's achievement.

One point of interest is that in the early drafts the novel is limited to family affairs. In one draft it is entitled *Two Marriages*, in another *Two Couples*. The guiding idea remained, indeed, the idea of the family; but in the early drafts the treatment is more detached, less personally committed. The highly autobiographical Levin does not even appear. The families contrasted are the Oblonskys and the Karenins. Later drafts bring in under various names the character finally called Levin; but even then Tolstoy at first concentrated on Levin's family life. It was only still later that he introduced the rich matrix of

[1] It seems very probable that the generally philanthropic purpose behind the *ABC Book* was blended with a polemic intention to assert the claims of morality, imagination and instinctive wisdom, against scientific method and the thirst for 'facts' (cf. Gradgrind). (See the interesting article by B. Eykhenbaum, 'Tolstoy posle *Voiny i Mira*', *Literaturnoye Nasledstvo*, *35–36*, Moscow, 1939, 221–64.)
[2] See N. K. Gudzy's excellent account in *JE*, *20*, 577–644.

Levin's speculations in philosophy and religion, and his social and economic aspirations. Concurrently, the novel as a whole grew in social reference till it became the great picture of an epoch, the Peace of the 1860s. The contrast between the families (now three) remained the core of the novel, but it was now set, and set with remarkable skill and significance, in the picture of society. For instance, Karenin, the ministerial machine, is both the perfect contributory cause of Anna's disintegration, and a most convincing specimen of a kind of official naturally engendered by the social conditions of the period.

This leads conveniently to a second point: in early drafts Anna is an unbeautiful, though attractive, coquette, streaked with sheer diabolism, narrow-minded and unintelligent. Karenin, though physically unattractive, is kindly and good-hearted. Vronsky is shown as fascinating, intelligent, and something of a poet. There is no hint of the Anna we know, with her incredible beauty and charm, her capacity for a great love, and her fundamental honesty; nor of the final Karenin, the dry bureaucrat, utterly unable to satisfy Anna's legitimate craving for genuine tenderness and passion. Nor is there in the Vronsky of the early drafts that element of a past among the *jeunesse dorée* of St. Petersburg, that strain of basic irresponsibility and egoism, to be found in the ultimate conception. It seems as if in the early drafts Tolstoy had forgotten his original idea of showing the unfaithful woman as pitiful and not guilty; and that it is only in course of composition that he recaptures it, evolving, in Anna, a character vulnerably unsatisfied, and, despite resistance, a prey to exploitation, and overmastery by passion. He even improves upon the original conception; for Anna is now a character who poignantly commands his love and respect, as well as his sympathy. There is, however, no doubt that Anna's passion is now for a man fundamentally unworthy of her. Tolstoy gives Vronsky, indeed, many decent qualities, and his final voluntary enlistment for the Serbo-Turkish War shows his substance. Besides, he increases in seriousness and responsibility in the course of the book, and only reverts to briar when Anna becomes unbearably possessive. All the same, Vronsky certainly never becomes truly worthy of her. The significance of this fact I shall suggest presently.

The excellence of the characterization in the novel as we know it is a commonplace of criticism. All the main characters are live and markedly different personalities, and the sure touch extends even to minor figures, such as the insufficiently egoistic Varenka and the ultimately frustrated intellectual, Koznyshev. Some of the characterization does, indeed, rely on tricks of technique, but these are very skilfully used. The physical realization of Karenin, for instance, is masterly. Tolstoy's trick of insistence on physical oddities and mannerisms, which becomes a little tiresome and even pointless in the celebrated instance of the protruding lower lip of Andrei's first wife in *War and Peace*, is admirably adapted to the satire on Karenin, both when it involves caricature (Karenin's habit of cracking his fingers) and when it directs attention to the right kind of physical repulsiveness (the thin official voice). The portrayal of Karenin, however, as of many of the other characters, does not rely to any considerable extent on such devices. It relies, in the main, on Tolstoy's firm sensitiveness to human impulses, and their fluxes and refluxes. In Karenin's case a striking instance is his 'conversion' to a charitable attitude towards Anna during her illness. This is not, I think, a mere survival of Tolstoy's original conception of Karenin, but a perceptive intuition that even a machine of a man like Karenin could react in such a way in such circumstances. It is also subtly seen by Tolstoy as not only temporary but a preparation for the passively stubborn and hypocritical role Karenin later plays under the aegis of Countess Lydia Ivanovna.

The excellent characterization is an achievement; but only an ancillary one. Only ancillary, too, is the splendid depiction of particular scenes, e.g. the horse-race, the mowing, the parting of Anna from Seryozha, or the séance with Landau the medium. But that such things can be only ancillary is a measure of the novel's stature. Tolstoy's main achievement here seems to me to lie, first, in the full artistic realization of the moral theme condensed in the epigraph from *Romans*: 'Vengeance is mine, I will repay'; secondly, in the elaborate contrast between the three families, and the profound and vigorous pondering of the question what a family should be like; and thirdly, in the searching description of the maladies of an epoch, as seen and felt by an intelligent, sensitive and passionate individual— Levin.

The realization of the central moral theme is a miracle of art. Anna's initial resistance, and subsequent capitulation to her repressed passion, the ebb and flow of her impulses, the conflict between her passion for Vronsky and her maternal feelings for Seryozha, the inimical working of an exclusive and hypocritical *grand monde*, the concurrent growth of possessiveness in Anna's attitude to Vronsky and of re-deployment of male interests in Vronsky, the ultimate turn of the screw, and Anna's brainstorm and death, are all recounted with unerring sensitiveness and unrelaxing force. Always, or at least almost always, Tolstoy accords the maximum of sympathy to Anna, and also makes her seem greatly superior to the society which plays such a large part in her destruction. This is all in accord with what seems to me to be the significance of the epigraph: that it is the announcement of a mystery, an indication of the working of divine laws, and, at the same time, a denial of any human right to cast the first stone.

Anna makes a fatal mistake in yielding to Vronsky; but the moral blame for it is highly attenuated. The book shows forth *inter alia* the highly probable results of a fatal error of that kind committed in a given state of society. To G. A. Rusanov, who complained that Tolstoy was cruel to give to Anna the end he did, Tolstoy's reply was that his heroes and heroines sometimes came to do things he would not have wished them to do, and that what they actually did was simply what they would do in life.[1] Given the character of Anna, and the character of Vronsky, and the circumstances delineated in the novel, this was probably true. And so we can say that Anna's end is both in accord with the central moral theme and also true to life.

Yet this is not the end of the matter. Tolstoy's answer to Rusanov was perhaps not completely satisfactory. For Tolstoy *chose* to depict just that character of Anna and that character of Vronsky and just those circumstances, and to bring that fine person, Anna, to that torture and death. This he deliberately chose to do; and he did so for the sake of vindicating the rigorous, unconceding view of marriage to which he tenaciously clung, and because he regarded irregular unions as more perilous and unsatisfactory than the repressions of the Karenin family. The book has a sharp polemic edge directed against the rise of a freer attitude to sex and marriage in the Russia of the 'sixties and 'seventies. Tolstoy struck hard in taking a woman with Anna's capacity for love and high spiritual and physical attractions, and showing that even in her case the move towards freedom would bring disaster. There was no need to add any blame. Tolstoy had cast the first stone himself in writing the novel. He had shown in full detail how what he considered to be God's law would bring such a woman to a terrible end.

[1] *Tolstovski yezhegodnik, 1912,* Moscow, 1912, 58; quoted by S. P. Bychkov, *L. N. Tolstoy,* Moscow, 1954, 294.

It is further possible to urge that, as a polemicist, Tolstoy, despite his appearance of fairness to adulterous love in deciding after all to take not a mere coquette but a fine person as his heroine, was perhaps really less than fair in making her lover considerably inferior. To have placed them both on a lower plane would, indeed, have made his polemic ineffective. It would always have been easily possible for his adversaries to deny that he had chosen a fair instance. But that procedure would, at least, have been crystal clear; whereas in *Anna Karenina* Tolstoy has, with evident deliberateness, tendentiously distracted attention from the possibility of a splendid individual achieving an ultimately satisfying love outside marriage—that is, from the most favourable case—while presenting a case which has some delusive appearance of fairness.

Tolstoy's execution of this tendentious purpose, on the other hand, is admirable. The convincingness of the central narrative is supported by the clear contrasts between the various couples. The Oblonskys, though in disorder, are evidently to be considered superior both to Vronsky and Anna, and to Anna and Karenin, in virtue of the vital fact that at least one of the partners is genuinely trying to fulfil the functions of a parent. Yet that parent is also shown as under stress and herself lacking in complete integration. It is only in Levin and Kitty that we find the makings of a satisfactory family; and even with them things do not run really smoothly.

These contrasts, it can be seen, also serve to explore the idea of a *family*, and thus the theme of Anna's adultery and the question of what a family should be like are interwoven.

Nor are the reactions of Levin to the problems of the period entirely detached from the rest of the novel. Such a family as Levin's could only function wholly satisfactorily within the framework of sound relationships between peasantry and landlord; and

71

Levin comes to doubt even the possibility of achieving these. He comes to see the interests of peasant and landlord as fundamentally opposed. The conflict adumbrated in *A Landowner's Morning* comes to be shown in *Anna Karenina*, for the first time, as the conflict between the ideals of a landlord and father, on the one hand, and those of one who recognizes the rights of men, on the other,—the conflict which was to have such a tremendous effect on Tolstoy's own life and on a number of his later writings.

As compared with *War and Peace*, *Anna Karenina*, despite many passages and even whole chapters abounding with *joie de vivre* and humour, is shot with a sense of disillusion, and at times clouded with pessimism. The premonitory accident to the railwayman soon after the outset, the death of Frou-Frou, the frustration and despair of Levin, and the ultimate collapse of Anna, create a darker atmosphere than all the terrible events which are absorbed into the epic world of *War and Peace*.

These two great novels are the greatest masterpieces of European fiction in the nineteenth century. They are, however, sometimes taxed with 'lack of unity', and with being 'realism run riot'. There may be some passages in both novels which would give colour to such strictures, but substantially the judgments only show failure to understand the works. There is, indeed, contradiction in *War and Peace*, and it is explainable by Tolstoy's changing ideas during composition; but this is not the 'lack of unity' which is usually complained of. The war passages and the peace passages seem to fall apart, the narrative is often disjointed, our attention is not concentrated for long on a single train of events, the philosophizing breaks up the story. These are the kinds of mistaken complaint that have often been urged. Again, in *Anna Karenina*, it is alleged we are just getting interested in the Oblonskys when we have to switch attention to the Karenins, and then this intrusive and tiresome fellow Levin intervenes and we are asked to follow his troubles and speculations which seem to have little to do with the main theme. Such objections are, in my view, not very substantial, and are easily answered. Both novels are in open form. They do not attempt tightly-knit stories with climaxes. They are both representations of life on a large scale. Moreover, they both have at least two kinds of unity which should override all complaints. The first is the unity deriving from the central theme. In *War and Peace* this is substantially the great defensive war against the predatoriness of military and political ambition. In *Anna Karenina* it is the theme of the family and of right relations between the sexes. The second is the unity afforded by the powerful personality of the writer, with his spirit questing for answers to deep moral problems and to important social and political questions, with his hawk-eyed observation and subtle introspection, his passionate and sometimes brutal sincerity, and his paradoxical mixture of malice and quarrelsomeness with expansiveness and good-will.

This is also part of the answer to the charge of 'realism run riot'. Tolstoy's realism in these novels is very seldom that of a mere observer. He is almost always strongly committed in one way or another, and the tone of the writing is charged with feeling. What is more, the feelings are often very powerful, and are also very various. This, among other things, sharply differentiates Tolstoy's realism from Flaubert's. If it be said, however, that even so there is too much of life in these novels—insufficient selection—by what criterion is the judgment being made? If part of the main point of a book is to give fairly full and free expression to the life and problems of a period, we should not be too readily tempted to say that the book contains too much life. Surely our only reliable criterion will then be the criterion of *worthwhileness*, not too pedantically construed? And according to such a criterion Tolstoy, with his intuition of significances and his lyrical vitality, very seldom fails.

1878–1910

> If people are going to occupy themselves with my writings, let them dwell on those passages in which I know that the Divine power spoke through me, and let them make use of them in their lives.
>
> Tolstoy's Will of 27 March 1895.

Soon after he completed *Anna Karenina* Tolstoy was overwhelmed with that sense of despair which brought about his moral crisis and 'conversion'. Thereafter his religious attitudes almost wholly dominate the fiction, and though sometimes he writes as a hierophant, and sometimes as a sinner, the moral religion behind the work is one and the same.

Many of the aspects of this religion are expressed with great intensity in many of the short stories he wrote, in simple style, for the people.[1] These almost all teach explicitly that the only life worth living is a life dedicated to God's will. Some teach what Tolstoy thought specifically followed from this. In *Two Old Men* the pilgrim who never reaches Jerusalem because he attends on the way to the misfortunes of a peasant family is shown to have acted better than the pilgrim who visits all the Holy Places. In *The Story of Ivan the Fool*, where Tolstoy makes great use of irony and shock-exposure of current military violence and capitalistic exploitation, the teaching is that the peaceful performance by every individual of his fair share of manual labour is a primary human duty, that money and soldiers are only instruments of egoistic ambition, and that military attack can be

---

[1] A number of these are translated in *Twenty-three Tales*, *CE*, *13*, and World's Classics.

conquered by non-resistance. *The Imp and the Crust* is a fanciful temperance parable. *How Much Land Does a Man Need?* is a powerful indictment of greed for land. One of the subtlest tales is *The Empty Drum*, an attack on state violence.

Some of these stories Tolstoy invented. Others are re-written folk-tales. Most of them have an urgency which springs from Tolstoy's poignant realization of the continual threat of death which hangs over everyone, and his fervent belief in the vital importance of Christian love and mutual help between all human beings. The texture and form of the best of the stories are supreme. The moral naturally grows out of the narrative, which is generally conducted with great skill: in some cases hurrying on with a grotesque rapidity reminiscent of Voltaire, in others moving with quiet care and earnestness; occasionally, too, dwelling for a moment, to gather power, on the physically horrifying or the nightmarish. Telling effect is often achieved by the familiar ballad and folk-tale technique of recounting episodes in series. The moral tendency of these stories, on the other hand, is open to criticism. Even the view that love and kindness are valuable whatever their consequences is not really so attractive as it might seem; but the exaggerated optimism as to the likelihood of the unkind being converted by the kind, hatred overcome by love, and violence by verbal reproach or passive resistance, is positively dangerous. Ivan was lucky to keep his kingdom. Such optimism was perhaps necessary for propagandic effect. It would not encourage love and kindness to show how often they fall on stony ground. But they do so far more often than Tolstoy's stories suggest.

Some of these popular tales actually sketch cases of conversion, but this theme is more elaborately treated in other works of the last period: *The Death of Ivan Ilych, Master and Man,* and the posthumous fragment, *Memoirs of a Madman.* The powerful

Memoirs have considerable biographical interest, but are not a work of art. The other two works are artistic wholes. In both the protagonist is converted, from egoism to love for others, under the stress of acute mental and physical agony in the face of impending death. It is well-nigh unbearable to read of the mounting torture of Ivan Ilych, the official who dies through a simple fall which occurred while he was re-decorating his new St. Petersburg home. Slightly less cruel because less monotonous is the suffering the reader has to endure as the egoism of the master Brekhunov is broken down during a bewildering nocturnal blizzard, and he comes to sacrifice himself by lying on the body of his servant to protect him from the cold, so freezing to death. The uncanny power of these narratives is undeniable. Indeed, especially in *Ivan Ilych*, it seems rooted in the pathological. Such experiences scarcely bear thinking of, and *in themselves* belong to those parts of life that are best not dwelt on, and, indeed, if possible, best forgotten. Tolstoy, however, does not dwell on them *for themselves*, but for the sake of his conception of Christian love. In this respect *Master and Man* seems the more convincing. Ivan Ilych could only too easily have died in despair. Brekhunov is faced with a definite choice, and his decision grows naturally from the situation. In both tales, however, the anguish springs from an unhealthy intensity, close to madness.

Another main theme of the longer fiction of the last period is the danger, and even hatefulness, of sexuality. This theme is the exclusive concern of *The Kreutzer Sonata* and of the two posthumous tales, *The Devil* and *Father Sergius*; and it is fused with the theme of spiritual regeneration in *Resurrection*. In *The Kreutzer Sonata* the highly-pitched outpourings of the hero, Pozdnyshev, who has murdered his wife, have a shrillness which approaches insanity. Tolstoy skilfully disowns this insanity, continually referring to Pozdnyshev's irritable excitability, and at one point even making him admit himself 'a sort of lunatic'. His opinions, however, Tolstoy does not disclaim, and, indeed, they are obviously the *raison d'être* of the book. Like Iago, Pozdnyshev dismisses as non-existent any love between the sexes, distinct from sensuality. Like Byron, another libertine, he is acutely sensitive to the sordid character of the marriage-market. Women are trained from childhood to capture men; and so they dominate society—through sensuality. The social consequences are far-reaching. 'All the luxuries of life are demanded and maintained by women. Women, like queens, keep nine-tenths of mankind in bondage to heavy labour.' Husbands like this sensuality and cultivate the sexuality of their wives. Sexual intercourse, however, in Pozdnyshev's view, is quite unnatural ('Ask a child, ask an unperverted girl'). To the question how the human race would continue without it, his retort is: Why should it continue? If life is for life's sake, there is no reason for living, and then Schopenhauer, Hartmann, and the Buddhists would be right in thinking we ought not to live, and should renounce the will to do so. If, however, life's aim is goodness, that would be more easily attained by stamping out the passions, and especially the strongest passion, sexual love. These positions of Pozdnyshev's are crucial, and, I think, basically unsound. If life were for life's sake, life would provide its *own* reason for living; or else it would *require no reason*. If, however, life's aim were goodness, it is unlikely that the extinction of the passions would achieve life's aim. It might be a greater achievement to attain goodness with the passions than without them; and for many it might be *impossible* without them to achieve goodness at all. But Pozdnyshev fails at other points too. Besides denying any love between the sexes distinct from sensuality, he dubs the sensuality 'something abominable, swinish, which it is horrid and shameful to remember'. Such a view as Pozdnyshev's is not surprising in one who started sexual life as he or Tolstoy did. But those sexual careers were misfortunes, and the doctrines engendered by them have no claims to the title of universally valid moral teaching. Even *were* sexual love nothing but sex, it would not follow that the sexual act is an act of shame. Much more could be said of the wild errors of Pozdnyshev's diatribes. But one would still have to admire the force of the writing, and the seriousness of the moral ideals behind it.

Similar horror at sex underlies *The Devil* and *Father Sergius*, but these are tightly-controlled narratives of specific cases. They do not make exaggerated generalizations; and they are compact. Yet they do not canvas such a range of aspects of sex as *The Kreutzer Sonata* does. *The Devil* is the powerful story of a landowner, Irtenev, who, at first 'for health's sake', and later under the spell of personal fascination, has clandestine sexual relations with the wife of a local peasant. After a time Irtenev marries a woman who makes an exemplary wife. The peasant woman's curiosity, however, and chance meetings, work on Irtenev till he becomes obsessed with her attractions. Even an absence of several months does not cure him, and, in a fit of despair, he kills himself, or, in an alternative version, the peasant woman. The suspense of the narrative and the close description of the stream of the landowner's tortured consciousness are masterly. One of the less obvious but highly Tolstoyan morals of the story is that a man who has sexual relations with a woman is responsible for her subsequent sexual life, so that if she grows loose he bears the guilt. The work is directly an attack on the irresponsible morality of some members of the landowning classes of that time; but its moral implications obviously do not rest there. As to the obsession, Tolstoy carefully points out that, though judicially Irtenev was pronounced insane, he was really on the same level of sanity as the general run of humanity. The implication is clearly that such sexual passion could attack and destroy *anyone*, and is not to be trifled with by such practices as indulging in sex 'for health's sake'. Yet the attitude to sex in this story is not so negative as in *The Kreutzer Sonata*. The possibility of an entirely satisfying marriage is not excluded, even though not actualized.

In *Father Sergius* Tolstoy tells the tale of an aristocratic Guards officer, who, when he learns that his fiancée has become the Emperor's mistress, renounces the world, and enters a monastery. The story deals with the subsequent spiritual development of Sergius, in particular relation to his resistance to sexual temptations. It is, in my view, a finer achievement than either *The Kreutzer Sonata* or *The Devil*. The sense of the nature of true spiritual progress is impressive. The positive values behind Tolstoy's repudiation of lust and sexual love are here recorded more clearly than in any of the fiction save *Resurrection*. The sequence of episodes, showing the subtle interrelation of pride and lust, is managed with the greatest skill, and the whole tale is outstandingly economical. Tolstoy was indeed justified when, after reading part of it to some friends, he exclaimed with closed eyes: 'The old man wrote it well!'

Tolstoy's third and last full-length novel, *Resurrection*, took even longer to mature than the first two. Once again the original conception was far narrower than the final creation. A. F. Koni, a celebrated jurist and magistrate, who was staying with the Tolstoys at Yasnaya Polyana in 1887, told Tolstoy the story of an orphan girl, adopted by a wealthy lady, but eventually seduced by one of that wealthy lady's young male relations. She became pregnant, and was expelled from the house. Left stranded by her seducer, she placed the child in an institution, tried to earn a living, failed, and became a prostitute. Sometime later she was arrested for stealing from a drunken visitor to the brothel. At the trial her seducer, by a strange coincidence, was on the jury. Deeply impressed with his own guilt, he resolved to marry the girl, who was sentenced to a short term of imprisonment. He did so, but she died soon after of typhus. The story struck Tolstoy deeply, and he suggested that Koni should write and publish it. A year later Koni had not done so, and Tolstoy obtained his leave to use the story. He did not, however, start at once. Not long after, in March 1889, he writes to G. A. Rusanov that he wants to write 'a broad free novel like *Anna Karenina*' in which he could express, without strain, what seemed to him 'a new, unusual, and useful slant on people'.[1] Eventually the two purposes coalesced, and 'The Koni story', somewhat modified, became the novel *Resurrection*; but Tolstoy did not finish it till more than ten years later. He made many attempts to settle to it, but either became dissatisfied or was diverted by other work— famine relief, the problem of decadent art, the development of his religious and political ideas, the writing of shorter works of fiction (e.g. *Master and Man*, *Father Sergius*, and *Hadji Murad*). Yet with each attempt the novel grew richer.

Resurrection is probably now generally underrated in Western Europe and America. It should be precious to us for one reason if for no other: that it is the only full-length work of fiction in which are embodied the ideas on life and society which are most characteristically Tolstoyan. The novel is potent both in its affirmations and in its rejections. The intense and plenary assumption of moral responsibility by the hero, Prince Nekhlyudov, is combined with the fiercest satire on the decadence and corruption of Tsarist administration in the 1880s, and on what Tolstoy took to be the sinister workings of the Russian Orthdox Church, the President of whose Holy Synod is scarifyingly attacked

[1] *Vestnik Yevropy*, 1915, No. 3, 15.

in the character of Toporov. Some idea of the sting of the writing may be gathered from the fact that only 25 out of 129 chapters were untouched by censorship.

Resurrection expresses in fictional form Tolstoy's decisive break with the political and social traditions and beliefs of his class, and with the form of Christianity practised within the established Church. It also expresses, fully and movingly, the moral implications, in a specific situation, of genuine belief in Christianity as Tolstoy understood it. The value we set on the novel will naturally vary with our attitudes to Tolstoy's religious, social, and political ideas. A convinced member of the Orthodox Church could scarcely set such store by the work as a practising Tolstoyan. Soviet critics, on the other hand, following Lenin, value the work for its powerful criticism of Tsarist rule—and indeed of 'reactionary' rule anywhere—while deprecating the work's advocacy of Christian love and non-resistance as a substitute for physical force.[1] In any case, however, the depth and importance of the attitudes expressed in the novel deserve recognition and admiration. As to form, in contrast with the earlier novels, a single subject and plot are undeviatingly followed, despite considerable variety of scene. There is, on the whole, less psychological analysis than before, and greater use of contrasting portraits of characters in action. The hand of the author is also more obvious. The writing is, for the most part, very forceful. The exposure of the farce of the pompous and utterly inhuman law court, of the egoism of public administrators, and of the empty artificiality of the life of the decadent nobility, is as strong satire as any in Tolstoy. He writes with the ruthlessness of a man sure of his convictions.

[1] See e.g. A. A. Ozerova in '*Roman Voskreseniye*' in *Lev Nikolayevich Tolstoy, Sbornik statei i materialov*, Moscow, 1951; and E. P. Andreyeva in '*Roman Voskreseniye*' in *Tvorchestvo L. N. Tolstovo*, Moscow, 1954.

Prince Nekhlyudov's moral rebirth and subsequent progress are also generally convincing. Katyusha Maslova, however, is not fully realized; nor is the pacifist and vegetarian, Simonson, whom, in Tolstoy's final version, Maslova marries.[1] Yet Simonson is a clear enough symbol of the kind of man on whom Tolstoy pins his faith for the future of humanity. He is a peaceful revolutionary, deeply sincere and filled with Christian forbearance. Being a revolutionary, he differs from Karatayev; and the difference corresponds to a difference of atmosphere between *Resurrection* and the earlier novels. *War and Peace* and *Anna Karenina* both included favourable descriptions of characters of the nobility living the life of their social class. *Resurrection* includes no such description. The life of the nobility is no longer seen to have a place in the best society. The *grand monde* is the great mass of the peasantry. Not, however, the proletariat. The book advocates nationalization of the land and the imposition of a single tax, according to the system of Henry George. That would have caused a drift back to the land. Tolstoy maintains to the end his hatred of large towns and their corrupting influences. In this respect *Resurrection* preserves continuity with *Anna Karenina*.

Though I greatly admire *Resurrection*, I suspect that it is factually exaggerated, and its ideals, though fine, seem to me mistaken. The mordant satire on the corruptions is acceptable; yet it is hard to believe in the implication that the best in the tsardom of the 1880s had nothing better to offer. It is also hard to believe in the greatly superior virtues of the Russian peasantry, and in Tolstoy's conception of their ideal social rôle. The best peasants were no doubt very fine people, and decency was probably widespread; but it by no means follows that the best social organ-

[1] Tolstoy wondered whether to make Nekhlyudov marry Maslova, but put the point to the test of a game of patience, which did not come out (Tolstoy to Goldenweizer, Feb. 1909).

ization would have been autonomous peasant communes. I share Tolstoy's love of the country and general dislike of large towns; but I cannot help thinking that premature resettlement on the land might delay an ultimate and more satisfactory resettlement. Again, a sense of responsibility in the ruling class, and, indeed, in every individual in every class, offers greater hope against oppression and distress than the breakdown of the class system, whether through voluntary capitulation by the ruling classes, as Tolstoy suggests, or through the violence of social revolution. Yet the social revolutionaries were right, as against Tolstoy, in believing that pressure from them was a strong factor in favour of social improvement. Whether, indeed, in the conditions *Resurrection* purports to describe, there was any hope of an increased sense of responsibility among the ruling classes of Russia remains a question.

One work of fiction completed by Tolstoy after *Resurrection* is of special value and interest: *Hadji Murad*, the tale of the Chechen chieftain who fought under Shamil, but, in revenge for his leader's hostility, the murder of his father and brother, and seizure of his wife and children, goes over to the Russians in hope of receiving command of an army with which to destroy his enemy. Owing to intrigue and delay, Hadji Murad does not get his army; and so flees from the Russians with the intention of recapturing his family by a bold coup, with the help of a few henchmen. The Russians pursue him and surround him in a swamp, where he goes down, fighting to the last. The verve of the narrative and the Homeric vividness of the detail are remarkable; and so is the fact that the converted Tolstoy should have written such a story. The full weight of Tolstoy's sympathy seems to be with the resistant mountaineer. Not a trace of the long-cherished philosophy of non-resistance or Christian forbearance, or even of self-perfection, is present. Certain other work written by Tolstoy in the late 'nineties and first decade of the new century has a similar character; but *Hadji Murad* is the best example of the tendency. Though Tolstoy recognizes Hadji Murad's love of power and thirst for gain, he lays stress on his deep family love, his daring, resolution, initiative, and longing for a free and full life. It is tempting to see here a re-assertion of Tolstoy's sub-conscious egoistic life-force against the oppressive claims of his stern conscience. There is an interesting diary entry for 5 August 1902: 'I have been writing on Hadji Murad, partly with pleasure, partly against the grain and with shame.' Whatever the biographical significance of the story, however, there is, in any case, something peculiarly satisfying in the spirit behind the work: the passionate love and care for life and its details, and for genuine strong natural impulses, untamed either by the hypnotic force of an effete civilization, by the ruthless despotism of a barbarian overlord, or by the inner workings of over-careful conscience. The story does indeed also contain, as we might expect from the author of *Resurrection*, a vitriolic exposure of the irresponsibility of Nicholas I and his ministers; but powerful as these episodes are in themselves one cannot but suspect them of exaggeration and unfairness, and this weakens their force. Some Soviet critics try to see also in the story propaganda for the union of all Caucasia with Russia, and a scorn of the reactionary Murid fanaticism which constituted some of Shamil's power over his followers.[1] I fail to find the first in the story at all, and the second seems at most present in a very mild degree. The story impresses one rather with the great threat to life and happiness which lies in the two contrasting despotisms of Shamil and Nicholas; with the poetic power of this wild and dangerous Caucasian life, rising at moments to a tragic intensity,

[1] See L. D. Opulskaya in 'Pozdneye tvorchestvo L. N. Tolstovo' (*L. N. Tolstoy, sbornik statei*, Moscow, 1955).

which several times finds expression in the poignant spell-binding old Caucasian songs; and by its compelling sympathy with the fine wild chieftain, tenacious of life to the last, hanging on like the red wild thistle, the only living thing in the field to survive the passage of the plough—the symbol with which Tolstoy begins his tale, and with which he ends it.

Generally, however, the fictional work of Tolstoy's last years embodies his religious convictions, sometimes with particularly striking artistry, as in the posthumous stories, *The Forged Coupon, After the Ball,* and *Alyosha the Pot. The Forged Coupon* is the remarkable story of the horrifying ramifications of an original misdeed by some schoolboys, followed by a corresponding narrative of the chain-reactions set up by an act of repentance, which ultimately lead to the spread of happiness. Tolstoy thought, with some justification, that he had here opened up a new form. It certainly admirably expresses the central conviction that the moral tendency of everything one does is vitally important. *After the Ball* tells first of a ball at which a young man dances for most of the evening with a girl of eighteen, intoxicated with love; and then of the shattering of that love the very next day when he sees the girl's father, a colonel, order the cruel 'gauntletting' of a deserter. The purposely brutal intensity of the contrast and the restrained force of the explicit moral indignation are superb. *Alyosha the Pot* is quite different. It is the miniature life-history of a good, simple boy, put upon by everyone, who dies young of an accident, but who, throughout his brief life, and right up to his death, has been actuated by nothing but serene resignation and good-will. It is a touching epitome of the human values Tolstoy had come most to admire.

A Review

Much of the art even of Tolstoy's first period is partisan, and some of its attitudes would have been acceptable to the converted Tolstoy, though others (e.g. profound respect for the modestly efficient soldier, patriotic fervour, admiration for bold love-making) would have seemed misplaced or superficial. The work of the first period, in any case, has no dominant world-view. Some of it, indeed, is not even partisan, but shows a fresh curiosity about life and its possibilities, and an interest and passion for nature and people just as they are. The same personal experience of a night journey through a blizzard,[1] which forms the tempestuous background to *Master and Man*, was forty years earlier the subject of a purely descriptive story, *The Snow Storm*. The work of the first period however, even where not partisan, is as alive with feeling as that of the other two, and, in general, more mercurial.

In the two great novels the range of interest and experience is immensely extended. Tolstoy has come to grips with the deepest moral, social, and political issues. Yet these novels stand closer to the first period than to the third. Their guiding ideas—the glory of a great defensive war, and the notion of family life, were to be alien to the later Tolstoy. And this is true also of many of the attitudes expressed in the course of the novels, e.g. the glorification of patriarchal landowning in *Anna Karenina*. Still more important, perhaps, is the impression, in both novels, of a ranging search of the world and human experience, which contrasts sharply with the certainties of the later work. The full sense of life and the temperamental character of the feeling are further links with the early Tolstoy. *Anna Karenina* is, indeed, nearer to the later work than *War and Peace*, but it comes before the great divide.

The short stories written by Tolstoy during the second period for his two *ABC Books* (his reading primers for Russian peasants) are, on the other hand,

[1] In January 1854, on his way home from the Caucasus on leave.

technically and sometimes spiritually very close to the work of the final phase.

That it is a gross mistake to think that Tolstoy ceased to be a great literary artist after his conversion is now widely recognized by critics. The work does, however, differ from what had gone before. Tolstoy's extraordinary powers of observation and introspection are not used so freely. They are governed by the ultimate moral or religious purpose, or by obsessional compulsion. And the feelings expressed, though intense, are more restricted in range. This is connected with the changes in form and style. The stories generally proceed without digression, and drive home the moral purposes they embody. The style is simple, firm and direct—even in works not primarily intended for peasant readers. Asides and exclamations, momentary reflections, and expressions of longings and urges and doubts occur scarcely at all. It is evidently a much changed man that is writing—a man with certainties to tell of rather than doubts and searches.

Throughout the three phases, and even in his parables, Tolstoy remains a realist. He faces life squarely, and draws it firmly. He seldom employs suggestion, and he never conjures with metaphor [1] or with words for their own sake. But he does not seek out the harsh, ugly or abnormal. He does not blink it, but it does not engulf his writing, as it often does Dostoyevski's. Tolstoy is in far closer contact with the normal life of his time than Dostoyevski, and perhaps, indeed, than any writer of fiction contemporary with him, except Leskov.

Tolstoy's realism, however, is never coldly observant, it is always emotionally committed, and, indeed, from first to last, combines strong positive and negative feeling. Tolstoy was a satirist to the end:

[1] For a short but suggestive study of Tolstoy's distrust of metaphor see Nina Gourfinkel, *Tolstoï sans Tolstoïsme*, Paris, 1946, ch. 3.

the indignation at the heartlessness of the plutocrats of the Schweizerhof is more than matched by the indignation at the brutality of the colonel in *After the Ball*. But Tolstoy also remained capable of the most passionate joy: in the description of the spring day in Moscow at the opening of *Resurrection* there is as strong an uprush of intoxicated feeling for nature as in the most lyrical outbursts in *The Cossacks*.

III

Formative Forces

Personalities and denunciations attract attention
more readily than ideas or artistic work, though were
it not for Tolstoy's opinions and works no one would
care how he lived.

Maude, *Life of Tolstoy.*

The chief thing for me is: not to feel guilty.

Levin in *Anna Karenina.*

Here I wish to indicate briefly a few aspects of Tolstoy's historical and personal environment, and of his
character, which seem particularly relevant for understanding his ideas and fiction.

Tolstoy's youth and early manhood were passed
under the bureaucratic regime of Nicholas I (1825–
55), whose repressive policy after 1848 undoubtedly
fostered the mistrust of government Tolstoy had
already acquired, partly under the influence of Rousseau, in his late 'teens. At Sevastopol this mistrust
turned to indignation. Tolstoy, who had himself
played a courageous part in the defence, was angered
by the contrast between the brave defenders and the
incompetent government and military leaders. His
anger is evident in the second and third Sevastopol
Sketches, but its effect reached further. His hatred of
the rule of Nicholas and his ministers was, as we have
seen, a basic drive of *War and Peace*, while in the
pungent satire on Nicholas in *Hadji Murad* political
hostility is reinforced by personal disgust. And Tolstoy's anger at Sevastopol probably had a powerful
influence on his general political views.

Tolstoy's attitude may also have owed something to his father's example. Boris Eykhenbaum
may be right in stressing the passage in Tolstoy's

Recollections [1] characterizing his father as something of a *frondeur*, who not only retired from government service on ideological grounds, but held aloof from intercourse even with local officials.

Tolstoy himself did, indeed, twice contemplate government service, and he served for five years in the Army; but in 1857 his horror and disgust at an execution by guillotine in Paris resulted in a vow never to serve any government.[2] His hostility was soon reinforced by other experiences, such as the police search at Yasnaya Polyana and on his Kursk estate in 1862, on a false report of revolutionary activities.

The fury of Tolstoy's mortal war against government during his last thirty years, however, might not have been so deadly had not the comparatively liberal rule of Alexander II been succeeded by the generally reactionary reigns of Alexander III (1881–94) and Nicholas II (1894–1917). These clinched Tolstoy's enmity; and even the moderate and intelligent rule of Stolypin after the election of the third Duma (Nov. 1907) was hateful to him.

Tolstoy was also disturbed by the rise of the capitalist *bourgeoisie*. At first he resented it as an upstart threat to the old landowners. He deplores the decree barring the nobility from trade. Later, in the 'seventies, moral distrust blends with his aristocratic resentment, as in the venomous portrait of the merchant Ryabinin in *Anna Karenina*. Later still, the aristocratic resentment, at least ostensibly, ceases, and Tolstoy condemns the capitalist class as self-seeking and corrupt, and a parasitic drain on the peasant masses.

Tolstoy was also much influenced, in this case positively, by an event three years before his birth: the abortive rising of the Decembrists in 1825. The

[1] Tr. *CE*, *21*, 19; cf. B. Eykhenbaum, *Lev Tolstoy*, I, Leningrad, 1928, 12.
[2] Letter to Botkin, 7 April 1857, tr. in *Tolstoy, Literary Fragments, etc.*, ed. R. Fülöp-Miller, New York, 1931, 232.

Decembrists were a lifelong symbol for Tolstoy of the possibility of initiating and achieving great social changes through a moral *élite* at the top of the social hierarchy renouncing their privileges for the good of society as a whole.[1] Tolstoy saw in their spirit the solution of what early became his own problem: how to live, with as complete moral satisfaction as possible, in a society in which he had inherited great privileges.

Tolstoy's inherited privileges were, indeed, perhaps the most important feature of his environment. Born a Count, he received on the division of the family property in 1847 Yasnaya Polyana and several smaller estates, about 1,960 desyatins (5,400 acres) in all, with 330 male serfs and their families. He soon contracted an uneasy social conscience; and it is no

---

[1] The Decembrists were for Tolstoy a lifelong symbol of this possibility, despite the fact that his preoccupation with them was only fitfully intense, and even despite certain changes in his attitude towards them. Tolstoy may have started a novel on the Decembrists in 1856, and he certainly did so in 1862 and again in 1878. Nothing of the first attempt is extant. The second led on to the writing of *War and Peace*. The third was broken off in 1879, apparently for two reasons: (1) because Tolstoy had been refused permission by the Chief of Police to work on the police records of the Decembrists (Letter of 3 Feb. 79 to Tolstoy from Countess Alexandrine Tolstoy, *Perepiska L. N. Tolstovo c gr. A. A. Tolstoy*, St. Petersburg, 1911, 310–11); (2) because he had discovered that the Decembrists were 'almost all French', meaning that they were acting under the influence of ideas which were French and that they were not rooted in Russia (*Memoirs* of Countess A. A. Tolstoy, ibid., 19 and cf. the *Reminiscences* of Tolstoy's brother-in-law, S. A. Behrs, *Vospominaniya o gr. L. N. Tolstom S. A. Behrsa*, Smolensk, 1893, 51 (quoted Bychkov, op. cit., 322); tr. C. E. Turner, London, 1893, 80–83; and P. A. Sergeyenko, *How Count Tolstoy Lives and Works*, tr. L. Hapgood, London, n.d. (1899), 11). It seems likely, moreover, that after his conversion Tolstoy could hardly have wholeheartedly approved of the violence which the Decembrists were prepared to use to achieve political changes. Nevertheless, despite his abandonment of the novel, and despite his new philosophy of non-resistance, we find many admiring references to the Decembrists in Tolstoy's later work, correspondence, and reported conversations.

gross exaggeration to say that he spent much of the rest of his life trying to pacify it. Tolstoy was never sufficiently grateful to his great-great-grandfather, whose treacherous part in the murder of the Tsarevitch Alexis had brought him the title of Count, and enabled him to found the family fortunes. Tolstoy ultimately owed to him not merely obvious debts, but most of the primary conditions for two of his greatest problems: the moral problem of his precise duties to his peasants, and the related social problem, the Russian land question.

The social problem, at least, was not peculiar to Tolstoy. In Russia between 1800 and 1860 land reform was a dominant question. The problem sprang from the large grants of serfs made to landowners in the eighteenth century, particularly under Catherine the Great. Despite liberal opinion, favouring emancipation, no overall solution was achieved under Alexander I or Nicholas I.

When Tolstoy received his property he left Kazan University, without taking his degree, to run his estates and improve the condition of his serfs. The serfs, however, were suspicious. He was unable to effect substantial improvements, and his enthusiasm flagged. But his concern with the problem remained, and inspired his projected *Novel of a Russian Landowner*.[1] After Sevastopol he again tried to solve his peasant problem. He offered to allow each peasant household 4½ desyatins (*c.* 12 acres) of land. The ½ desyatin was to be a free gift. For the other 4 desyatins the peasants were to pay 5 roubles a desyatin for thirty years. Tolstoy was to use one rouble to discharge a mortgage on his estate. The other 4 would be the purchase money. The peasants considered the plan, but rejected it. They had heard that Alexander II, when crowned, would free the serfs and give them all the land. When Tolstoy said that if he gave them his land he would be left without his shirt, they laughed.

[1] See p. 53, above.

In 1861 came the Emancipation, formally freeing all serfs, and allowing them to buy small plots from their former masters with money or labour. Controversies were to be settled by district Arbiters. Tolstoy was appointed for his district, and generally upheld peasant rights against unscrupulous landowners. These made life difficult for him, and after a year he resigned. This experience helped to make Tolstoy hostile to landowners, and to form his ultimate view that no land should be privately owned.[1]

Meanwhile, however, Tolstoy married (1862), and for some fifteen years energetically administered his estates, and, indeed, purchased fresh land to help provide for his rapidly increasing family. Not till his great moral crisis in 1878 did he come to feel disgust for landowning. Yet he had often felt perplexed about the peasants and the land problem, and this is reflected in *Anna Karenina*.

When Tolstoy lost faith in landowning, the Emancipation seemed to him a mere fraudulent replacement of personal by economic slavery. In 1884 he read Henry George. George advocated land nationalization, and a tax on each parcel equivalent to the yield, taking account of fertility and nearness to a market, but not of labour. Land would then have been controlled by those who worked it. Tolstoy thought this solution insufficiently radical, yet a practical compromise, which the Tsar could introduce by decree. He advocated it for the rest of his life, though without success. His belief in George's system lies behind *Resurrection*.

[1] This ultimate belief appears in countless pages of the later writings, but was expressed with particular pith in a conversation with S. Semyonov (winter 1894–5). (See Maude, *Life of Tolstoy*, World's Classics, II, 340–1.) Tolstoy had, however, expressed such a belief much earlier, for instance in a notebook entry for 1885 in which he quotes with approval *La propriété, c'est le vol*. But such beliefs lay underground for much of his early married life.

Meanwhile the city-ward drift continued, though many peasants migrated to Siberia. Tolstoy condemned the growth of the proletariat, whom he regarded as displaced peasants; but was exhilarated by resettlement in uncultivated areas, and more than once considered writing large-scale fiction about it—for instance, a sequel to *Resurrection*, showing Nekhlyudov settling with a peasant community on untilled land, and helping to work it with his own hands.[1]

In the late 'seventies Tolstoy had begun to neglect estate management, and to pay more attention to the personal difficulties of his peasants. In 1891 he divided his property between his wife and children. But he went on living with his wife till shortly before his death; and his eventual flight from home may well have been due to his continual dissatisfaction at the discrepancy between his published views on property and his comfortable life.[2]

In any case, Tolstoy lived, thought, and wrote, for over sixty years, as the landowning, and then estate-sheltered, nobleman with an acutely active social conscience.

These influences might have made Tolstoy a secular revolutionary, but other influences worked to-

[1] Tolstoy was also fascinated by a similar idea much earlier. After he had prepared the second edition of *Anna Karenina* (in 1877) he turned again to work on a novel of the time of Peter the Great—this time with a quite new conception: instead of concentrating on 'high' society, he was now concerned with the masses at an important epoch of Russian historical development. The scene was to be set in 1723, and in Part II he was to describe a Russian Crusoe settling on new land on the Samara steppes, and beginning a new life. (Such a situation was, in actual fact, far more typical of the 1870s than of the early eighteenth century!) Again in 1877 Tolstoy introduced the idea of settlement in Irkutsk or Samara into his new conception of *The Decembrists*.

[2] This dissatisfaction was doubtless accentuated by the receipt of letters from time to time taunting him with not practising what he preached.

wards making and keeping him a profoundly religious man. Some of the people he loved most dearly were very religious: his mother, his aunt Countess Alexandra Osten-Saken, his favourite 'aunt' of all, Tatyana Alexandrovna Yergolski,[1] his cousin Countess Alexandra Andreyevna Tolstoy,[2] and his sister Marya. His early reading also played a great part. Besides the Sermon on the Mount the most powerful influences were Rousseau's *Confessions* and *Émile*. The religious views of Rousseau and Tolstoy are strikingly similar. Both base religion on reason. Both regard it as a way of life, though neither is a mere moralist, but each insists on the religious relationship between each individual and the infinite as the true basis of morality. Both accept the moral teaching of the Gospels, but repudiate miracles and salvation by faith, and deny the importance of ritual. Both reject incomprehensible dogmas. Both consider true Christianity fundamentally antagonistic to social values. Tolstoy is more radical about non-resistance, and in his denial of the use of adhering to local ritual, but in religion, as in so much else, his debt to Rousseau can scarcely be overestimated. Tolstoy read more widely than Rousseau, making, in later life, serious contact with the thought of China, India, and Islam;[3] but these influences supplemented Rousseau without replacing him.

All these forces helped to foster and maintain religious impulses in Tolstoy, even during his bouts of dissoluteness in youth and early manhood, and to lead

[1] In 1903 Tolstoy writes in his diary: 'A truly chaste woman who gives up the whole force of a mother's self-sacrifice to the service of God—of men—is the best and happiest human being (Aunty T.A.)'.
[2] Tolstoy considered his correspondence with her the best source of information for his spiritual biography.
[3] See Biryukov, *Tolstoi und der Orient*, Berlin, 1925; and for Tolstoy's study of Chinese thought, the excellent short book by Derk Bodde, *Tolstoy and China*, Princeton U.P. and Oxford, 1955.

him, progressive though he was, to oppose secular liberalism and socialism.

Against both religion and social conscience there ran the influence of dissolute, vain, and egoistic acquaintances at school and university in Kazan, and later in Moscow and Petersburg, and in the Army. Tolstoy's early diaries are full of clashes between religio-moral and egoistic attitudes. Symbolical is his behaviour when his brothers first took him to a brothel. When he had 'accomplished this act', he stood by the woman's bed and wept. Violent remorse also followed countless further indulgences during the next twenty years, and he developed that fear of the sexual attraction of women so frequently expressed in his works. Eventually he came to have a general horror of dissoluteness, and in his writings it always gets scant mercy. Moreover, no personal experience enabled him to sympathize with highly developed *liaisons* like that of Turgenev and Madame Viardot, or such as Anna Karenina might have had with a truly worthy lover. His early diaries also show him often actuated by crude forms of vanity and egoism, learned in fast company; and rounding on himself for being so. In course of time he left these behind, but, though his work shows acute insight into vanity and egoism, he never seems to have shed them completely. Gorki recounts how the *barin* in the septuagenarian Tolstoy could disconcertingly reassert himself. And there is other evidence.

Tolstoy was, in any case, a complex man, vital and passionate, yet persistently analytical, and sternly moral. It was often his vitality that led him as a young man into vanity and egoism, and his passion that in those early years sometimes degenerated into dissoluteness. Moreover, it was the sapping of his vitality and passion that paved the way for his 'conversion', in which and its aftermath his exacting conscience and his analytical power also played their part.

One heavy blow to Tolstoy's vitality and confidence in life was the death of his consumptive brother Nicholas at Hyères in 1860. Tolstoy had been deeply attached to Nicholas since childhood, when Nicholas had hidden at Yasnaya Polyana the green stick on which was written the wonderful secret which would make all human beings love one another and free them forever from all evil and misery. Nicholas died in Tolstoy's arms, and Tolstoy thought he expressed, a few moments before death, a convulsive terror of annihilation. This experience threw Tolstoy off his balance. A month later he writes: 'Nothing in my life has so impressed me. It is true, as he said, that nothing is worse than death. And when one reflects well that *that* is the end of all, then nothing is worse than life. Why strive or try, since of what was Nicholas Tolstoy nothing remains his?' [1]

Consolation, however, soon came to Tolstoy. He began to believe that immortality was a moral necessity. He then regained his balance, and began to find life bearable and interesting again. Most of the next eighteen years were filled with activity: the practice and theory of educating peasant children, marriage and domestic life, farming, writing *War and Peace* and *Anna Karenina*. Yet already in 1862, just before his marriage, Tolstoy exhibits hypochondria. Tired, and discouraged with his work as Arbiter and educationalist, he began to think himself mentally unsound, and also consumptive. Had he not felt there was still a possible source of happiness—marriage—he might have succumbed to despair. This time his balance was restored by a *kumys* cure in Samara.

The next difficult time came after his great effort on *War and Peace*. He was exhausted, and an easy prey to pessimism. By a fatal attraction he was drawn to Schopenhauer, whom he acclaimed as 'the greatest

[1] Letter to Fet, 10 Oct. 1860.

genius among men', and proposed, with his friend Fet, to translate into Russian. I strongly suspect that Schopenhauer helped to precipitate Tolstoy's next breakdown. He was, however, also disturbed by reading Greek literature, in which he found moral ideas utterly opposed both to his early Christian education and to the *Profession de foi du Vicaire Savoyard*. He again became melancholy, and was again saved by a *kumys* cure in Samara, in the summer of 1871.

The worst, however, was yet to come. During the next few years Tolstoy was frequently faced with suffering and death, including the suffering and death of offspring and other close relations. *Anna Karenina*, which he worked at intermittently during those years, shows signs of nervous strain and morbidity in places. Tolstoy himself assigned the start of his great breakdown to 1877, but it seems to have begun in 1875, and to have gathered force in bouts of melancholia of increasing intensity, culminating in 1878. Tolstoy was 'much obsessed by death', and, *consequently*, found life bitterly futile and terrible. He had often had fits of depression after excesses in youth and early manhood, but this melancholia lasted longer, and was deeper and heavier and more terrifying. Moreover, his belief in immortality had faded.

He sought a remedy, and after failing to find it in science, secular philosophy, or the easy-going Epicureanism frequent among his class, he found it in religion—at first in the church-going religion of the peasants, who impressed him by their capacity to live, work, and die without *vertige*, but later, when further experiences and investigation led him to reject many Church dogmas, in what he considered the Christianity of the Gospels. Tolstoy's subsequent devotion to the cause of the great peasant masses of Russia probably derived some of its tenacity from his having owed to them and their religion his salvation from despair, while the sustained sharpness of his polemic against official Christianity undoubtedly stemmed from his conviction that its dogmas had been a hindrance rather than an aid to his deliverance. Furthermore, his contempt for the pretentions of science, and, to a lesser degree, of much secular philosophy, probably drew some of its venom from his awareness of their failure to help him at the decisive moment.

How far Tolstoy's great breakdown was due to fatigue and the pressure of circumstances, and how far to the assertion of feelings of guilt it is hard to estimate, but it seems clear enough that it was made more pervasive and more prolonged, as well as more profound, by his outstanding capacity for psychological and philosophical analysis. What is also certain is that the religion which delivered him from his desperate situation was one which made illimitable demands on him for good works. It required from him the renunciation of his wealth and privileges, and of all personal ambitions. It required from him the refusal to be a party to any form of coercion, such as war, government, or the forms of justice. Subsequently it demanded from him that he should cease to hunt or eat meat. Still later, it required of him that even in marriage he should aim at the ideal of chastity. And it also demanded from him that he should persuade as many people as possible to adopt the same kind of religion. Yet, on the whole, he seems to have regarded all these demands on him as not merely legitimate but divine. It was this religion, after all, that had delivered him from despair. What is more, in time this religion again allowed him to believe in immortality, and as this belief grew on him his fear of death seems to have more or less permanently disappeared.[1]

I hope that it is by now clear that it is a profound mistake to think, as some critics have done (e.g.

---

[1] Gorki represents Tolstoy as in continual fear of death; but this is against the weight of the evidence.

99

Mereschkowsky, Shestov, Thomas Mann), that Tolstoy's 'conversion' and the preaching of his subsequent years were somehow 'gratuitous'—a 'mistake' of a man who had no good cause to be so perverse. A typical pronouncement is that of Mann:

> 'This process of making a Christian and a saint of himself, on the part of a human being and artist so loved of nature that she had endowed him with godlikeness, was, as an effort at spiritual regeneration, most inept. Anglo-Saxondom hailed it with acclaim, but, after all, the spectacle is painful rather than gratifying, compared with Goethe's high endeavour.'

Mann maintains that, in contrast, the 'sick' Dostoyevski had good cause to aim at sainthood. But the truth is that Tolstoy himself was 'sick'—not, indeed, so sick as Dostoyevski, or, on the other hand, as Nietzsche, but sick enough for a radical change of attitude to life to be necessary. Goethe's attitudes and views may, admittedly, be more generally inspiring and even valid for healthy people; but this was in large measure because Goethe was fortunate in remaining healthy in his maturity, whereas Tolstoy's psyche suffered very severe shocks indeed, and was rendered incapable of the degree and continuity of joy in the things of this world that for Goethe remained possible.

That Tolstoy's way out of his despair should have been what it was is not surprising in view of early personal influences, the powerful effect on him of the Gospels, his attachment to Rousseau, his position of privilege, his wildness as a young man,[1] and his severe conscience. Yet it has no claim to universal validity, even as an antidote to despair. But once he had found a faith which enabled him to live and die, Tolstoy's rigorous intellect drew out its implications, and he rejected violently all attitudes which seemed to enable people to live and die without the faith he

[1] Cf. Bacon: 'And dissolute men become friars.'

himself held. He hated not only the attitudes of Nietzsche and the Darwinians, but also, for instance, those implied in much of Shakespeare,[1] whom, in this respect, he distrusted much as Pascal distrusted Montaigne.[2]

Tolstoy continued, on the whole, to derive fundamental peace from his faith, though he was deeply disturbed by political and social violence and oppression, and by growing disharmony with his wife. When depressed he now *longed* for death—and felt guilty in doing so! One secret of this change, though possibly only a symptom of something deeper, is his fresh acceptance of some form of immortality.

A little needs saying about Tolstoy's relations with his wife. When they married he was thirty-four, and she eighteen. With great honesty he asked her to read his diaries. She was horrified at his earlier sexual activities, and his earlier attachments made her morbidly jealous. She also found country life rather boring after Moscow. The couple had tiffs. Yet they settled to what was, for fifteen years, a generally happy and flourishing family life. Tolstoy wrote *War and Peace* and *Anna Karenina*, Sonya looked after the rapidly increasing family and worked as his secretary, and both managed the estates. But the famine of 1873 sharply stirred Tolstoy's social conscience, and at his great crisis (1878) one of his chief thoughts was the contrast between the 'godly' life of the peasant masses and the egoistic life of his own class. He longed to renounce exclusive pleasures and privileges, and live for 'others', which chiefly meant the great peasant population.

Sonya was distressed at Tolstoy's neglect of farming, and she understandably opposed attempts to practise his new faith. Nor did she like his working on Christian doctrine or writing political and social

[1] See *Shakespeare and the Drama*, CE, *21*.
[2] Cf. e.g. Pascal, *Pensées*, Éd. de la Pléiade, 838–9.

pamphlets, instead of producing fiction. Conflict was also caused by her increasingly violent fits of jealousy, and then her own compensatory passion for the pianist Taneyev. Sonya also resented the growing number of Tolstoy's disciples, who encouraged his beliefs, and encroached on his time. Perhaps the greatest cause of disruption was V. G. Chertkov, aristocrat and former Guards officer, who came to Tolstoy in 1883, gradually gained an ascendancy over him, struggled against Sonya for Tolstoy's copyrights, and eventually, helped by Tolstoy's daughter Alexandra, persuaded Tolstoy to execute a will virtually making him his literary executor. Tolstoy maintained sexual relations with Sonya till he was well over seventy, and frequently showed real affection almost till the end, but he was often cold and cruel to her, and came to regard sex as a means of enslavement to the egoistic life he wished to renounce. *The Kreutzer Sonata* was inspired by this attitude. Yet Tolstoy acknowledged Sonya to be the ideal 'pagan' wife—faithful, energetic, assiduously attentive to the material interests of the family. Where he thought she failed him was as a spiritual companion.

If we find Tolstoy's doctrines of universal love, and rejection of sex and family interests ultimately unattractive, we can greatly sympathize with Sonya, despite her steady refusal to give Tolstoy's views due weight. In any case Tolstoy's whole achievement rested on a contradiction. For he owed not only subject-matter but the material conditions for writing to conduct of his ancestors, and of himself in early years, directly opposed to his later teaching. If he had not felt guilty of maintaining his privileges he might, indeed, have lacked the urge to publish his message, yet had he entirely forgone them he might well have had no leisure to deliver it.

Life with Tolstoy would inevitably have involved hard times, because he was constitutionally com-

bative. This was clear to his schoolfellows and fellow
students at Kazan, his friends and acquaintances in
the Army and the literary world, his wife and near
relations, and himself. It is important, since it per-
vades most of his writings, though not always obviously. Tolstoy may have wished to reject the trait;
but he was a natural fighter and a natural satirist.

A few words about philosophical and literary influences. Tolstoy, a great reader, acknowledged
many such influences at various times. On his beliefs
and conduct the paramount influences were the
Gospels and Rousseau; but Schopenhauer and Eccle-
siastes seem to me to have weighed heavily on him at
a critical time; and he was also impressed (though not
so disastrously as Kleist) by Kant's scheme of the
limits of knowledge, and his proof that the existence
of God was indemonstrable. Pascal's *Pensées* com-
forted him greatly in 1876-7 with the hope of immortality, and he always admired and loved them.
But many other influences on his thought are readily
traceable: in politics, for instance, despite reservations, Herzen and Proudhon; in economics, Ruskin
and Henry George. Later came Eastern philosophy,
especially Confucius, Lao-tse, and Buddhism, but
also modern Muslim thinkers, and the contemporary
Indian religious teachers, Ramakrishna and Vive-
kananda.

As to more specifically literary influences, very
early there was Sterne, and Dickens, especially *David
Copperfield*, and, among Russian writers, Pushkin,
Gogol, Lermontov, Turgenev, Druzhinin, and
Grigorovich. Slightly later, and ultimately recognized by Tolstoy as the greatest *literary* influence,
came Stendhal, especially *La Chartreuse de Parme*. In
later life Tolstoy came to see in Dickens a great force
urging men towards universal brotherhood. Turgenev, on the other hand, then appeared too aesthetic; though at the end Tolstoy prophesied greater

permanency for Turgenev than for Dostoyevski, because of his superior 'art'.

Tolstoy's attitude towards Dostoyevski was curious. He evidently admired *The House of the Dead* quite early, but refers little to Dostoyevski until two years after his 'conversion' (and a year before Dostoyevski died), when we find him an enthusiastic admirer. Soon, influenced by his friend Strakhov's life of Dostoyevski, he began to have reservations. His later comments are mixed, but in 1901 he named Dostoyevski as among the five greatest Russian writers—the others being Pushkin, Lermontov, Gogol, and Herzen[1]; and I sense Dostoyevskian influence in *Ivan Ilych*, *Father Sergius*, and *Resurrection*.

When Tolstoy started writing fiction for the people he consciously simplified his style. He drank in the style of Old Testament stories, especially that of Joseph, which seemed to him the masterpiece of popular narrative art; and he steeped himself in the Lives of the Saints, and in Russian and foreign folk legends, not only for the matter but for the style. He also listened to the people themselves. In the summer of 1881, for instance, when he was finishing *What Men Live By*, he spent many an hour walking along the main Kiev road, talking with pilgrims and other travellers, and then noting down expressions which particularly struck him.[2] Tolstoy's love of the vivid and colourful in the speech of the people is also evident in works not primarily intended for them, such as *The Cossacks*, *War and Peace*, *Anna Karenina*, and, perhaps especially, *Hadji Murad*.

The influence of popular speech on Tolstoy, however, is really an influence by life rather than by litera-

[1] A. B. Goldenweizer, *Talks with Tolstoi*, tr. Koteliansky and Woolf, London, 1923, 70. It is perhaps worth adding that Tolstoy was reading *The Brothers Karamazov* during the night on which he left Yasnaya Polyana for the last time.

[2] *Countess S. A. Tolstoy's Diary*, tr. A. Werth, London, 1928, 70–1.

ture. But life was, in any case, the most potent of all influences on Tolstoy. He watched people sharply. He read history closely and penetratingly, and pursued searching inquiries into the lives of individuals who had died within living memory. He was acutely aware of his own stream of consciousness, and analysed it mercilessly. While it would be a great mistake to think of Tolstoy as free from the influence of other writers, in respect of beliefs, modes of thinking and feeling, and forms of expression, it would be a still greater mistake to underrate the pressure, on him and on his work, of life in its variety and power. Certain it is that Tolstoy profoundly distrusted literature which was too inventive; and he also intensely disliked work in which human content was sacrificed for verbal pyrotechnics, for the play of metaphor, for symbolism, for neatness of form, for anything intruding between the reader and the human experiences and problems which he rightly took to be the primary stuff and basic concern of all literary art.

CONCLUSION

Tolstoy's thought represents in an extreme form the drive towards freedom from interference. An abnormally intense urge towards freedom was perhaps congenital in Tolstoy. It may be symbolical that his first memory was of irritation at the constriction of his swaddling-clothes.

Tolstoy expresses this basic drive perhaps as forcefully and extensively as it has ever been expressed. He was not only a great handler of language but a powerful analyst, subtly and boldly drawing a host of conclusions from his basic premises. This in itself makes his non-fictional work still worthy of attention.

But these writings also sharpen our awareness of some of the more important problems of living. No one who reads *A Confession* or *What I Believe* or *What Then Must We Do?* or *On Life*, or *What is Art?* or *The Kingdom of God is Within You* is ever likely to forget the impression, or to view in the same way again the problems discussed. And these are as great now as they were then. *What Then Must We Do?* for instance, sprang from an acute situation in late nineteenth-century Russia; but its problems arise for every society, capitalist or otherwise.

The seriousness and fine texture of the thinking in these works are deeply impressive, and many of them are also works of art—most obviously *A Confession*, with its simplicity, economy, and restrained passion, but also works in more open form, such as *What I Believe*, *On Life*, *What is Art?* and *The Kingdom of God is Within You*.

As to the fiction, though we can understand how Tolstoy could come to depreciate *Childhood* and *War and Peace*, it would be absurd to accept his condemnation. Even if we thought the attitudes behind *Resurrection* or *Master and Man* or *The Death of Ivan Ilych*, finer than those behind the earlier work, the worth of underlying attitudes is not the only criterion of literary value. Moreover, the same attitudes—of the necessity to atone for wrong done, and of the importance of love for others and self-sacrifice, are sometimes present earlier, e.g. in *War and Peace*, *A Landowner's Morning*, *Lucerne*, and *The Cossacks*; and other attitudes found in earlier writings need have caused no shame to the later Tolstoy. Yet, admittedly, they were jumbled together with disparate and even conflicting attitudes—egoism, whimsical scepticism, a taste for 'triviality', the worship of vitality, admiration for resistance. The critic who said in the 'sixties that Tolstoy had no definite point of view was right. Indeed, up to and including *Anna Karenina* we find fundamental doubts and questions, and attitudes conflicting both among themselves and with Tolstoy's later views.

But doubts and questions are not necessarily worse than certainties and answers, nor are conflicting attitudes necessarily inferior to a single clear-cut posture. There may be more wisdom in the 'chaotic' changes of outlook in *The Cossacks*, or the dialectic of doubts and half-certainties in *War and Peace*, than in the unified and certain world-view behind *Resurrection* or *The Death of Ivan Ilych*; though the attitudes underlying the later work are fine enough to command most serious consideration, and from their point of view the earlier doubts and questions were only demands for *their* answers.

As to style and form, the linear economical writing of *Father Sergius* or *The Death of Ivan Ilych* or *Resurrection* or the tales for peasants has a strong attraction, and it is easy to see how the late Tolstoy came to see 'trivialities', mere descriptions, and the expression of floundering thoughts, as a waste of writing. Yet the victory of Tolstoy's urge towards order, economy, and linearity over his tendencies to expansiveness, digression, description for its own sake, and personal intrusion, should not be regarded as a triumph, but as entirely neutral for an evaluation. We should be grateful for the expansiveness of *The Cossacks* and *War and Peace* and even of *Youth*, and not deny it in a worship of economy and linearity. For Tolstoy himself, however, such a denial was not absurd, and without it we might not have had such fine examples of stricter writing as *Father Sergius* and many of the short stories.

What should be our overall estimate of Tolstoy's fiction? Its subject-matter, wide in range as it is, has nevertheless its limits. But Tolstoy writes of some of the most important kinds of situation of his time, and of all time, and any restrictions are, in any case, amply compensated by the authenticity of the writing. Time and again one feels that this has all been *lived*, or else *known* so well in essence (as in *Polikushka*) that the projection is perfect. And the situations are almost always precisely realized, felt into, felt through. The sense-impressions are often astonishingly vivid, the psychological observation uncannily faithful to even momentary shifts. Also, from first to last, sometimes wholly sane, sometimes daemonic and even tormented, there is moral aspiration, a passionate persistence to find a forward way out of evils and difficulties. And it is served by an alert diagnostic and critical power. Often, too, there is religious feeling, fitful in the early work, steadily sustaining in the later. Again, power of philosophical analysis—power to discuss *issues* searchingly—is evident time and again, though more frequently in the first two periods. And this rich matrix of the work is made richer by the power of Tolstoy's humour. In the earlier work this is often not particularly bitter or satirical; while in the work of the Christian Tolstoy it is more generally stinging and merciless. These characteristics all make for fine work; but they do not exhaust the wonders of Tolstoy's fiction. Contrary to the view of some critics, Tolstoy has a remarkable sense of form—of the most satisfactory embodiment of what he wants to say. The form is sometimes simple and strict—for instance, the binary or diptych form of *Two Hussars*, sometimes strict but more complex, as in *Childhood*, sometimes loose and complex, as in the two great novels. *Childhood* and *War and Peace*, and to a less degree *Anna Karenina*, were innovations in form. Tolstoy knew this, and indeed regarded innovation in form as characteristic of the best art. He considered, for instance, that *War and Peace* could not be called a novel, an epic, a history, or, indeed, anything but itself.

Is it as thinker or as artist that Tolstoy has greater claims upon us? The question may imply a false dichotomy. I have already suggested that Tolstoy is an 'artist' in his philosophical writings. He is also a 'thinker' in his fiction. In *Childhood*, in the Sevastopol Sketches, in *The Cossacks*, in *War and Peace*, *Anna Karenina*, *Resurrection*, he is forever wrestling with ultimate problems: the meaning of life, the meaning of war, how one should live, what social justice is, which is the ideal life of a family, what is the right relation of the sexes. Sometimes there is explicit discussion; at other times the issues and the answers (where found) are implicit. Taken in one sense, then, the question whether Tolstoy has more claim upon us as thinker or as artist leads to a dead end. If, on the other hand, what is being asked is whether Tolstoy's fiction or his philosophical works are the more important for us, my own answer would be that they are of equal importance—and I say this in spite of profound disagreement with some of his chief positions as a thinker. It is, I believe, important to emphasize the value of Tolstoy's non-fictional work at the present time; for, owing partly to accidental circumstances, partly to the Russian Revolution, the two wars, the spread of new philosophies, and other factors, they are in danger of being undeservedly neglected. They have much to teach us—even if all they teach us is how to disagree with them.

1828	28 Aug. old style (9 September new style). Born at Yasnaya Polyana (Province of Tula).
1830	Mother dies.
1837	Father dies.
1841	Move to Kazan.
1844	Enters Kazan University.
1847	Leaves University without taking a degree.
1849	Passes two examinations at Petersburg University.
1851	Goes with Nicholas Tolstoy to Caucasus. Serves as volunteer in Army. Nov. At Tiflis; writing *Childhood*.
1852	Joins Army.
1852–3	Campaigning in Caucasus. Writing *Boyhood* and stories of army life. Starts *The Cossacks*, and plans and starts *The Novel of a Russian Landowner*. Outbreak of Crimean War.
1854	Receives commission. Nov. In Sevastopol and area.
1855	Serving in area Sevastopol. Writes Sevastopol Sketches, and starts *Youth*. Nov. Returns to Petersburg.
1856	Jan. Death of Dmitri Tolstoy. Writes *Two Hussars*. Contemplates marriage with Valerya Arseneva. Nov. Leaves Army. Finishes *A Landowner's Morning*.
1857	Visits France, Switzerland, and Germany. Continues *The Cossacks*. Writes *Lucerne*.
1858–9	Alternating between Yasnaya and Moscow, with visits to Petersburg. Continues *The Cossacks*. Writes *Family Happiness*.
1859	Winter. Organizes school at Yasnaya.
1860–61	Apr. Visits Germany, France, Italy, England, and Belgium. Starts *Polikushka*.

1860	Oct. Death of Nicolas Tolstoy at Hyères.
1861	May. Quarrel with Turgenev.
	June. Appointed a District Arbiter of the Peace.
	Autumn. Resumes school work.
1862	May. Resigns from office of Arbiter.
	May and June. In Samara for *kumys* cure.
	Sep. Marries Sofya Andreyevna Behrs, daughter of a Court physician. Finishes *The Cossacks and Polikushka*. Shuts school.
1863–9	At Yasnaya, with visits to Moscow. Writing *War and Peace*.
1869	First reads Schopenhauer.
1869–70	Studies drama.
1870–71	Winter. Studies Greek.
1871	In bad health. *Kumys* cure in Samara.
	Sept. Starts work on *ABC Book*.
1872	Re-opens school.
1873–7	Writing *Anna Karenina*.
1873	Jul. Samara Famine.
1874	Death of Aunt Tatyana.
1875	Death of Aunt Pelageya.
1878	Great moral crisis and 'conversion'.
1879–83	Intensive theological study.
1879	Writing *A Confession*.
1881	Murder of Tsar Alexander II. Tolstoy appeals to Alexander III to pardon murderers.
1882	Buys house in Moscow.
1883	Writing *What I Believe*.
	Refuses jury-service.
	Meets V. G. Chertkov.
1884	*What I Believe* banned.
1885	Visits Crimea.
	With Chertkov and others founds *The Intermediary* publishing concern, for supplying reading-matter for the peasants. Writes stories for *The Intermediary*.
1886	Finishes *What Then Must We Do?* and *The*

Jubilee celebration of Tolstoy's birthday.
Writes articles on violence and capital punishment.

1908–9 Growing conflicts between Chertkov and Tolstoy's wife.

Quarrels of Tolstoy with his wife. Tolstoy keeps Secret Diary.

1909 Writes educational articles. Makes wills. Correspondence with Gandhi.

1910 Compiles *For Every Day* and *The Path of Life*.

July. Signs last will. Oct. Leaves home.

9 Nov. old style. Dies at Astapovo (Province of Ryazan).

Buried at Yasnaya Polyana 'at the place of the green stick'.

CHIEF WORKS, WITH DATES OF PUBLICATION

114

1891	*A Critique of Dogmatic Theology* (at Geneva) (wr. 1880–4)
1892	*A Union and Translation of the Four Gospels* (at Geneva) (wr. 1880–4)
1893	*The Kingdom of God is Within You*
1894	*Christianity and Patriotism*
1895	*Master and Man*
1898	*What is Art?*
1899	*Resurrection*
1902	*What Then Must We Do?* (at Geneva) (finished 1886)
	What is Religion?
1904	*Bethink Yourselves!*
1906	*Shakespeare and the Drama*
1908	*I Cannot be Silent!*

Posthumous:

The Porcelain Doll (wr. 1863)
Memoirs of a Madman (wr. 1884)
The Devil (wr. 1889)
Father Sergius (wr. 1890–8)
Hadji Murad (wr. 1896–1904)
The Forged Coupon (wr. 1899–1904)
The Live Corpse (wr. 1902)
Recollections (wr. 1902–8)
The Posthumous Notes of Fyodor Kuzmich (wr. 1905)

In addition there are notably many short stories, some of which are collected in English translation under the title *Twenty-three Tales*.

A Brief Note on some of the Russian Work on Tolstoy, 1928–1960. (For further work up to 1968 see pp. 127–8.)

The most important recent contribution to Tolstoy studies has been the Jubilee Edition of Tolstoy's Works, published in Moscow. Publication of this edition started in 1928, and was completed in 1958. The edition is in ninety volumes. It includes carefully edited texts of the fiction, sometimes markedly divergent from the texts hitherto published in Russian or in translation. It also includes drafts and variants, with scholarly textual commentaries, which facilitate genetic interpretation, and so help towards understanding the works in their final form. Another feature of the edition is the inclusion of a wealth of letters, and diary and notebook entries, many of which had not been published before.

Quite apart from the Jubilee Edition, an immense amount of work has been done on Tolstoy in Russia since 1928, the centenary of Tolstoy's birth.

A number of unpublished texts and other important original material were published in Moscow in 1939 in two large volumes entitled *Literaturnoye Nasledstvo. L. N. Tolstoy, 35/36, 37/38*, which also contain some excellent critical articles. Other collections of articles have also been published, perhaps the most important being *Lev Nikolayevich Tolstoy. Sbornik statei i materialov*, ed. D. D. Blagoy and others, Moscow, 1951, which also includes some unpublished texts and letters. Another very useful collection is *Tvorchestvo L. N. Tolstovo, Sbornik statei*, ed. M. B. Khrapchenko and others, Moscow, 1954. A somewhat more popular collection is *L. N. Tolstoy, Sbornik statei*, Moscow, 1955. Recently a large number of Tolstoy's pronouncements on literature have been assembled from scattered articles, letters, and diary entries (*L. N. Tolstoy. O Literature. Stati, Pisma, Dnevniki*, Moscow, 1955).

Several important full-length biographical and

critical works have been written. N. N. Gusev (at one time Tolstoy's secretary), who had already written a life of Tolstoy covering the period 1828–77 (*Zhizn L. Tolstovo*, 2 vols., Moscow, 1927), has since compiled an invaluable day-to-day chronicle of Tolstoy's life (*Letopis zhizni i tvorchestva Tolstovo*. Moscow–Leningrad, 1936), and more recently has produced a very detailed account of Tolstoy's early years (*Lev Nikolayevich Tolstoy. Materialy k biographii s 1828 po 1855 god*, Moscow, 1954) and of the period 1855–69 (*Lev Nikolayevich Tolstoy. Materialy k bio-graphii s 1855 po 1869 god*, Moscow, 1957). B. M. Eykhenbaum, a formalist critic, had earlier written an important two-volume bio-critical study of Tolstoy in the 'fifties and 'sixties (*Lev Tolstoy*, Vol. I, Leningrad, 1928; Vol. II, Moscow, 1931). More recently S. P. Bychkov has written a general survey of Tolstoy's whole life and work (*L. N. Tolstoy*, Moscow, 1954).

There have also been many shorter studies, both of Tolstoy's whole literary career and also of individual works or aspects of Tolstoy's achievement. Notable among the general accounts are two by N. K. Gudzy, one of the team of editors of the Jubilee Edition (*Lev Tolstoy*, 2nd enlarged edition, Moscow, 1944; and *L. N. Tolstoy, Iz kursa lektsii po istorii russkoy literatury XIX veka*, Moscow, 1952). N. K. Gudzy has also written an intensely interesting collection of studies of particular works and drafts of Tolstoy, which throw considerable light on his manner of working (*Kak rabotal Tolstoy*, Moscow, 1936). V. Shklovsky had written a formalist critique of *War and Peace* (*Material i stil v romane Lva Tolstovo 'Voina i Mir'*, Moscow, 1928), while more recently *War and Peace* has been the subject of a monograph by S. I. Leusheva, *'Voina i Mir' Tolstovo*, Moscow, 1954. Another note-worthy book is that of L. Myshkovskaya (*L. Tolstoy. Rabota i stil*, Moscow, 1939), which contains full-length studies of *Hadji Murad* and *Strider*, and a detailed account of the style of the peasant stories and of Tolstoy's later style in general.

Collections of older criticism on Tolstoy have also been published (e.g. *L. N. Tolstoy v russkoy kritike*, ed. S. P. Bychkov, Moscow, 1949; and the collection of Lenin's writings on Tolstoy, *O Tolstom, literaturno-kriticheski sbornik*, ed. V. M. Friche, Moscow–Leningrad, 1928); and reminiscences of Tolstoy by his contemporaries (e.g. *L. N. Tolstoy v vospominani-yakh sovremennikov*, Moscow, 1955, and V. F. Bulga-kov, *L. N. Tolstoy v posledni god yevo zhizni*, Moscow, 1957, 2nd. edn., 1960).

Other relevant works appeared in 1957–60 includ-ing: T. L. Motyleva, *O mirovom znachenii L. N. Tol-stovo*, Moscow, 1957 (an elaborate book on Tolstoy's innovations in world literature, and the influence of his work on writers of certain foreign countries); V. A. Zhdanov, *Tvorcheskaya istoriya Anny Kareninoy, materialy i nablyudeniya*, Moscow 1957 (a monograph on the literary history of Anna Karenina); V. T. Plakhotishina, *Khudozhestvennoye masterstvo L. N. Tol-stovo v romane Voskreseniye*, Kiev, 1958 (a critical study of *Resurrection*); L. M. Myshkovskaya, *Masterstvo L. N. Tolstovo*, Moscow, 1958 (an expansion of her earlier book including an essay on the literary history of *War and Peace*). And N. N. Gusev has brought out a second edition of his chronicle of Tolstoy's life, con-taining important new material *Letopis zhizni i tvorchestva Tolstovo, 1828–1910*, ed. L. D. Opulskaya, Moscow, 1958–60.

For further bibliographical information see *L. N. Tolstoy, 1828–1910*, ed. E. N. Zhilina, Leningrad, 1960.

SELECT BIBLIOGRAPHY
(compiled 1958; for further material to 1968
see pp. 127–8)

A. EDITIONS OF TOLSTOY'S WORKS

In English:

1. *Works*, tr. L. and A. Maude (The Centenary Edition), 21 vols., Oxford, 1928–37. (Referred to in the footnotes as *CE.*) (An excellent translation of many of the most important fictional and non-fictional works, with Aylmer Maude's *Life* [see F.1, below].)

The Maude translations of a number of the works are reprinted in The World's Classics.

2. *Works*, tr. Leo Wiener, 24 vols., Boston and London, 1904–5. (An accurate translation which includes some of the works not translated in *CE*, but does not contain others.)

3. Ed. R. Fülöp-Miller, *New Light on Tolstoy*, Literary Fragments, etc., tr. P. England, New York and London, 1931. (Includes material not available in English elsewhere—notably the three chapters of *The Decembrists*.)

4. *Stories and Dramas, hitherto unpublished*, tr. L. Turin, London and New York, 1926.

5. Some of the fiction is also available in other translations, e.g. in the Everyman Library and in Penguin Translations. Some other short works, mainly pamphlets, were published by The Free Age Press, Christchurch, and at Maldon in 1899–1902. Other pamphlets are: *The Crisis in Russia* and *The End of the Age*, London, 1906; *The Hanging Czar*, London, 1908; *Tolstoy on Land and Slavery*, Glasgow, 1909; *On Insanity* and *On Socialism*, London, 1936.

In Russian:

6. *Works*, ed. V. G. Chertkov and others (The Jubilee Edition), 90 vols., Moscow, 1928–58.

(Referred to in the footnotes as *JE*.) (The definitive Russian edition.)

7. *Complete Literary Works* (*Polnoye sobraniye khudozhestvennykh proizvedenii*), 15 vols., Moscow, 1928–30.

8. *Complete Literary Works* (*Khudozhestvennaya literatura Tolstovo*), 14 vols., Moscow, 1951–4. (With useful short commentaries on each of the works, based on the Jubilee Edition.)

9. A large number of cheap reprints of separate works are available, and a new edition of the literary works in 12 vols. is in course of publication (*Sobraniye sochineni*, Moscow, 1958–).

B. TOLSTOY'S DIARIES

In English:

1. 1847–52, tr. C. J. Hogarth and A. Sirnis, London, /n.d./, /1917/.

2. 1853–7, tr. L. and A. Maude, London, 1927.

3. 1895–99, tr. Rose Strunsky, New York, 1917.

4. 1910, tr. A. Maude in *The Final Struggle*, London, 1926. (See E.4, below.)

In French:

5. 1853–65, tr. J. Chuzeville and W. Pozner, Paris, 1926.

6. 1898–1910, tr. N. Rostowa and M. Jean-Debrit, Geneva, 1917.

In Russian:

7. All the extant diaries have now been published, with commentaries, in *JE*.

Note—Tolstoy did not keep a diary from March 1865 to March 1878. Not much of the diary for 1878–87 is extant; but the diary for Nov. 1888–Nov. 1910 exists, and very little of it has yet been translated into English.

C. NOTEBOOKS

These contain miscellaneous notes, including notes for works, observations on nature, people, and books. They have not yet been translated into English.

In Russian:

1. All the extant notebooks have now been published in *JE*.
2. Interesting extracts were published in *Literaturnoye Nasledstvo*, 37–8, Moscow, 1939.

D. LETTERS

About 8,000 of Tolstoy's letters are extant. Many, especially early ones, are known to have been lost. Especially interesting are his correspondences with the following: his wife Countess S. A. Tolstoy, his cousin Countess A. A. Tolstoy, his friends A. A. Fet, N. N. Strakhov, A. I. Herzen, L. D. Urusov, V. V. Stasov, V. G. Chertkov, M. K. Gandhi. Very little of this material exists in English. We have, however:

1. *The Letters of Tolstoy and his cousin Countess Alexandra Tolstoy (1857–1903)*, tr. L. Islavin, London, 1929. (A fairly large but incomplete selection.)
2. *Tolstoy's Love Letters* (to Valerya Arseneva), 1856–7, tr. S. S. Kotelianzsky and V. Woolf, London, 1923.

Some letters are also included in A.3, above; and letters are liberally quoted in F.1, 2, 9, 11, and 12, below.

In French there are notably:

3. Léon Tolstoï, *Lettres*, Paris, 1902. (A small collection.)
4. *Correspondance Inédite de Léon Tolstoï*, tr. and ed.

J.-W. Bienstock, Paris, 1907. (Mainly philosophical, political, and economic.)

5. *Tolstoï par Tolstoï, avant sa crise morale* (*1848–79*), *Autobiographie épistolaire*, tr. and ed. E. Halpérine-Kaminsky, Paris, 1912. (A well-chosen and well-edited collection of 135 letters.)

6. *Lettres à Botkine*, tr. and ed. J.-W. Bienstock, Paris, 1926.

7. *Lettres à Charles Salomon*, tr. and ed. J.-W. Bienstock, Paris, 1931.

8. Léon Tolstoï, *Lettres*, tr. and ed. B. Goriely, I (1842–60), Paris, 1954.

(A very useful collection of 125 letters.)

A number of Tolstoy's early letters were actually written in French. There are also many French translations of letters in the French translation of Biryukov's *Life* (see F.12, below).

All Tolstoy's extant letters have now been published in Russian in the Jubilee Edition. A fair number of partial collections also exist in Russian.

E. REMINISCENCES OF TOLSTOY BY HIS FAMILY AND CONTEMPORARIES

The following are available in English:

1. *The Diary of Tolstoy's Wife*, 1860–91, tr. A. Werth, London, 1928.

2. *Countess Tolstoy's Later Diary*, 1891–7, tr. A. Werth, London, 1929.

N.B.—Countess Tolstoy's diary for 1898–1909 is not available in English.

3. *The Autobiography of Countess Sophie Tolstoy*, tr. S. S. Koteliansky and L. Woolf, with Preface and Notes by V. Spiridonov, London, 1922.

4. Count S. L. Tolstoy (son), *The Final Struggle*, containing Countess S. A. Tolstoy's Diaries for 1910,

with extracts for the same year from the Diaries and Reminiscences of Leo Tolstoy, V. F. Bulgakov, D. P. Makovitski, A. B. Goldenweizer and others, and all the important correspondence for 1910, tr. A. Maude, London, 1936.

5. S. A. Behrs (brother-in-law), *Recollections of Count Tolstoy*, tr. C. E. Turner, London, 1893.

6. Count I. L. Tolstoy (son), *Reminiscences of Tolstoy*, tr. G. Calderon, London, 1914.

7. Count L. L. Tolstoy (son), *The Truth About My Father*, London, 1924.

8. *Family Views of Tolstoy*, tr. L. and A. Maude, London, 1926. (Articles on various aspects of Tolstoy and his activities by members of his family and friends.)

9. T. Kuzminskaya (sister-in-law), *Tolstoy as I Knew Him*, London, 1948.

10. A. P. Sergeyenko, *How Count Tolstoy Lives and Works*, tr. I. Hapgood, London, 1899.

11. A. B. Goldenweizer, *Talks with Tolstoi*, tr. S. S. Koteliansky and V. Woolf, London, 1923.

12. V. G. Chertkov, *The Last Days of Tolstoy*, tr. N. Duddington, London, 1922.

13. M. Gorki, *Reminiscences of Tolstoy, Chekhov, and Andreyev*, tr. K. Mansfield, S. S. Koteliansky, and L. Woolf, London, 1934.

The following in French are of particular interest:

14. Countess A. L. Tolstoy (daughter), *Ma Vie avec mon Père*, tr. A. Pierre, Paris, 1938.

(There is also an incomplete English version of the same work—by E. Varneck, London, 1933.)

15. T. L. Suchotina (daughter), *Journal*, with intr. by A. Maurois, Paris, 1953.

(There is also an incomplete English version, T. Sukhotin-Tolstoy, *The Tolstoy Home*, tr. A. Brown, Columbia U.P., and London, 1951.)

The best biographies in English are:

1. A. Maude, *The Life of Tolstoy*, 2 vols. (included in A.1, above, also reprinted in World's Classics, Oxford, 1930).
2. E. J. Simmons, *Leo Tolstoy*, London, 1949.

The following are also noteworthy:

3. R. Rolland, *Tolstoy*, tr. B. Miall, London, 1911. (A fine appreciation.)
4. G. R. Noyes, *Tolstoy*, London, 1919.
5. H. I'A. Fausset, *Tolstoy: The inner drama*, London, 1927. (An interesting psychological study.)
6. Thomas Mann, 'Goethe and Tolstoy' in *Three Essays*, tr. H. T. Lowe-Porter, New York, 1929, London, 1932, and reprinted in Mann's *Essays of Three Decades*, tr. H. T. Lowe-Porter, London, 1947. (A brilliant long essay.)
7. A. I. Nazarov, *Tolstoy, the Inconstant Genius*, London, 1930.
8. G. Abraham, *Tolstoy*, London, 1935. (A well-written brief life.)
9. D. Leon, *Tolstoy, his Life and Work*, London, 1944. (A full-length bio-critical work, somewhat less punctilious as biography than the works by Maude and Simmons, but sensitive and intelligent, with useful critiques of many of Tolstoy's works.)
10. S. Zweig, *Adepts in Self-Portraiture* (Casanova, Stendhal, Tolstoy), tr. E. and C. Paul, London, 1952. (Containing a brilliantly written psychological portrait of Tolstoy.)
11. Countess A. Tolstoy (daughter), *Tolstoy: A Life of My Father*, London, 1953. (Contains some material not previously available in English.)

In French the following are worth mention:

12. P. Birukov, *Tolstoï: Vie et Oeuvres*, tr. J.-W. Bienstock, 3 vols, Paris, 1906–9, 4th vol., Paris, 1923.

(The 'official' biography, the first three volumes of which were seen and criticized by Tolstoy. N.B.—The English translation is a much truncated version.)

13. M. Hofmann et A. Pierre, *La Vie de Tolstoï*, Paris, 1934. (A perceptive short life.)

14. F. Porché, *Portrait psychologique de Tolstoï*, Paris, 1935. (A longer biography, with a psychological slant—very French.)

The following works in German are noteworthy:

15. R. Löwenfeld, *Tolstoi, sein Leben, seine Werke, seine Weltanschauung*, 2nd. edn., Berlin, 1902.

16. Th. Mann, *Goethe u. Tolstoi, zum Problem der Humanität*, Berlin, 1932. (A slightly varying version of 6, above.)

17. K. Hamburger, *Leo Tolstoi—Gestalt u. Problem*, Bern, 1950. (An excellent study of several aspects of Tolstoy's personality.)

G. CRITICAL STUDIES

(See also F.1, 2, 3, 9, 12, 14, 15, 17, above.)

1. M. Arnold, 'Count Leo Tolstoi', first publ. 1887, reprd. in *Essays in Criticism*, 2nd Series.

2. W. D. Howells, in *My Literary Passions*, New York, 1895.

3. D. S. Merezhkowsky, *Tolstoy as Man and Artist: with an essay on Dostoïevsky*, Westminster, 1902. (An interesting but exaggerated essay, not wholly faithful to the spirit of Tolstoy or of his work.)

4. P. Kropotkin, in *Ideals and Realities in Russian Literature*, London, 1905.

5. M. de Vogüé, in *The Russian Novel*, tr. H. A. Sawyer, London, 1913.

6. T. G. Masaryk, in *The Spirit of Russia*, New York, 1919.

7. G. Wilson Knight, *Shakespeare and Tolstoy*, London, 1934.

8. J. Lavrin, *Tolstoy: an Approach*, London, 1944 (2nd edn., 1948).

9. D. S. Mirsky, in *A History of Russian Literature*, London, 1949.

10. G. Lukacs, in *Studies in European Realism*, tr. E. Bone, London, 1950.

11. G. Orwell, in *Shooting an elephant, and other essays*, London, 1950.

12. G. H. Phelps, in *The Russian Novel in English Fiction*, London, 1956.

Among the older Russian critiques the following deserve special mention:

13. N. N. Strakhov, *Kriticheskiya Statii o Turgeneve i Tolstom*, St. Petersburg, 1895.

14. N. K. Mikhaylovski, articles on Tolstoy, reprd. in *Sochineni N. K. Mikhaylovskovo*, St. Petersburg, 1897, Vol. VI.

15. K. N. Leontiev, *O Romanakh Gr. L. N. Tolstovo, Analiz, stil i Vlyaniye*, Moscow, 1911.

16. V. V. Veresayev, *O Dostoevskom i Tolstom*, Moscow, 1911.

Space precludes reference to many useful books and articles on special aspects of Tolstoy. A few of these have, however, been mentioned in the footnotes.

Addendum:

After this book first went to press there appeared: R. G. Hare, *Portraits of Russian Personalities between Reform and Revolution*, London, 1959. This book, the fruit of close contact with Russian sources, contains two interesting chapters on Tolstoy.

SUPPLEMENTARY BIBLIOGRAPHY (to 1968)

EDITIONS

Sobraniye sochineni, ed. N. N. Akopova, N. K. Gudzy, N. N. Gusev, M. B. Khrapchenko, 20 vols., Moscow, 1960–65. (A handy, well-edited and briefly annotated edition.)

Lev Tolstoy ob iskusstve i literature, ed. K. N. Lomunov, 2 vols., Moscow, 1958. (A collection of Tolstoy's opinions on art and literature.)

Writings on civil disobedience and non-violence, tr. A. Maude, London, 1960.

Further editions of translated fiction have appeared, e.g. in The Everyman Library (with Introductions by N. Andreyev), and in Penguin Translations.

LETTERS *Correspondance de Tolstoï avec Biriukov*, tr. M. Sémenoff, Paris, 1957.

Correspondance de Gandhi et Tolstoï, tr. M. Sémenoff, Paris, 1958.

Perepiska s russkimi pisatelyami, ed. S. Rozanova, Moscow, 1962.

(A very useful collection of over 500 letters to and from Russian writers.)

REMINISCENCES

P. Boyer, *Chez Tolstoï*, Paris, 1950.

T. L. Tolstoï (Soukhotine), *Sur mon père*, Paris, 1960.

Count S. L. Tolstoy, *Tolstoy remembered by his Son*, tr. M. Budberg, London, 1961.

BIOGRAPHY

A. Alexandre, *Le Mythe de Tolstoï*, Paris, 1960.

Lady Cynthia Asquith, *Married to Tolstoy*, London, 1960.

B. M. Eikhenbaum, *Lev Tolstoy, 70-ye gody*, ed. B. I. Bursov, Leningrad, 1960.

N. N. Gusev, *Lev Nikolayevich Tolstoy: materialy k biographii s 1870 po 1881 god*, Moscow, 1963.

M. Hofmann and A. Pierre, *By Deeds of Truth*, tr. R. W. Fernand, London 1959 (tr. of F. 13).

S. Laffitte, *Léon Tolstoï et ses contemporains*, Paris, 1960.

B. S. Meilakh, *Ukhod i smert Lva Tolstovo*, Moscow, 1960.

H. Troyat, *Tolstoy*, tr. N. Amphoux, London, 1968. (Tr. of *Tolstoï*, Paris, 1965.)

127

CRITICISM

N. N. Ardens (N. Apostolov), *Tvorchesky put L. N. Tolstovo*, Moscow, 1962.

J. Bayley, *Tolstoy and the Novel*, London, 1962.

I. Bounine, *La délivrance de Tolstoï*, Paris, 1939.

B. I. Bursov, *Lev Tolstoy: ideynye iskaniya i tvorchesky metod, 1847–62*, Moscow, 1960.

B. I. Bursov, *Lev Tolstoy i russky roman*, Moscow, Leningrad, 1963.

I. V. Chuprina, *Trilogiya L. Tolstovo 'Detstvo', 'Otrochestvo' i 'Yunost'*, Saratov, 1961.

R. F. Christian, *Tolstoy's 'War and Peace', A Study*, Oxford, 1962.

B. I. Kandiev, *Roman epopeya L. N. Tolstovo 'Voina i mir', kommentary*, Moscow, 1967.

M. B. Khrapchenko, *Lev Tolstoy kak khudozhnik*, Moscow, 1963.

G. V. Krasnov, *Geroy i narod v romane L. N. Tolstovo 'Voina i mir'*, Moscow, 1964.

Literaturnoye Nasledstvo, 69, Moscow, 1961.

A. A. Saburov, *'Voina i Mir' L. N. Tolstovo*, Moscow, 1959.

E. J. Simmons, *An Introduction to Tolstoy's Writings*, Chicago, 1968.

G. W. Spence, *Tolstoy the Ascetic*, Edinburgh and London, 1967.

G. Steiner, *Tolstoy or Dostoevsky; an essay in contrast*, London, 1960. (With revisions, Harmondsworth, 1967.)

L. N. Tolstoy, *Sbornik statei o tvorchestve*, ed. N. K. Gudzy, Moscow, 1959.

Tolstoy-khudozhnik; sbornik statei, Moscow, 1961.

N. Weisbein, *L'Évolution Religieuse de Tolstoï*, Paris, 1960.

V. V. Yermilov, *Tolstoy khudozhnik i roman 'Voina i Mir'*, Moscow, 1961.

V. V. Yermilov, *Tolstoy-romanist*, Moscow, 1965.

E. Y. Zaidenshnur, *'Voina i mir' L. N. Tolstovo; sozdaniye velikoy knigi*, Moscow, 1966.

V. A. Zhdanov, *Tvorcheskaya istoriya romana L. N. Tolstovo 'Voskreseniye'*, Moscow, 1960.

V. A. Zhdanov, *Ot 'Anny Kareninoy' k 'Voskreseniyu'*, Moscow, 1967.